"This book marks the 'leaving home' of family therapy. Charlés has achieved the Promethean task of breaking those chains that tie family therapy practice to specific cultural contexts and has provided a pragmatic and personal account of its application to international contexts. This exquisitely crafted book consists of a wide-ranging series of almost poetic essays (and engaging stories) that cover everything a multilateral family therapist needs to know when working across borders and in conflict ridden states. The book includes many gems of wisdom including innovative ideas for role-plays and suggestions about how training can be adapted to allow family therapy to reach its full international potential in ameliorating human suffering. Within all of this lies Charlés singular passion for increasing the resilience of the family however it is construed in the cultures where she has worked."

—*Mark Rivett, director of Systemic Studies, University of Exeter, UK*

"This exceptional book takes us on a journey through multilateral systemic practices. Being both an experienced practitioner in family therapy and a qualitative researcher, Dr. Charlés looks at her humanitarian work from an almost autoethnographical perspective. We follow her reflections with keen attention and curiosity, learning practically along the way. She puts into our backpack theoretical knowledge, safety instructions, models and stories to learn from as well as visions for the future. If this journey were a Grand Tour, Dr. Charlés would be our bear-leader!"

—*Professor Dr. Maria Borcsa, Institute of Social Medicine, Rehabilitation Sciences and Healthcare Research, University of Applied Sciences Nordhausen, Germany*

"In this comprehensive and engaging book about international family therapy, Laurie Charlés captures the wrenching complexities, sustainable possibilities, and moral hazards of offering mental health services on the global stage. She writes informally, as if chatting with you on a flight to Kosovo or Lebanon or Sri Lanka, but her stories and musings reveal the breadth and depth of her political savvy and international experience. A sophisticated multilateral thinker, Charlés's illuminations draw on her expertise as a qualitative researcher and systemic clinician, supervisor, and trainer. Soon into the book, you'll find yourself wanting to renew your passport."

—*Douglas Flemons, Ph.D., LMFT, professor emeritus of family therapy, Nova Southeastern University, USA*

"Working as a Peace Corps volunteer alongside Dr. Charlés many years ago, I recall her thoughtfulness when planning projects. She already understood that foreigners can't save a community and always ensured that her work was sustainable. In this book, Dr. Charlés effectively sets the stage for the reader by defining and explaining complex ideas such as gross national happiness, states, and international human rights law. She describes so clearly the multiple layers involved in working internationally in the mental health field. Her personal experience along with her expert knowledge is a perfect combination that makes for a must-read for every person planning to work in any realm of healthcare internationally."

—*Sara Cross, M.D., infectious diseases physician; associate professor of medicine, University of Tennessee Health Sciences Center, USA; Returned Peace Corps Volunteer, Togo, West Africa, 1999–2002*

INTERNATIONAL FAMILY THERAPY

International Family Therapy brings the international plane and its emphasis on the global community of states to systemic family therapy.

Informed by a coherent, multilateral perspective, each chapter covers a specific topic, including: discussions on the basis of state sovereignty and the role of international human rights law; the concept of human security and psychosocial risk to vulnerable populations; and the international economics and trade of public mental health initiatives for families across the globe. Written in an accessible style and peppered with vignettes and descriptive case examples, the text encourages the reader to better understand and implement family systems approaches from the perspective of the international system, with a focus on cultural considerations and best practice throughout.

Combining key theoretical tenets of family therapy and essential knowledge of international relations relevant to global mental health, *International Family Therapy* is an essential guide for family therapy practitioners interested in working internationally.

Laurie L. Charlés, Ph.D., LMFT, implements systemic family therapy practice in international humanitarian relief contexts, in low- and middle-income countries, and with vulnerable populations in conflict-affected states. She is the author or co-editor of several books on family therapy, most recently, *Family Therapy Supervision in Extraordinary Settings: Illustrations of Systemic Approaches in Everyday Clinical Work*, with Dr. Thorana Nelson.

INTERNATIONAL FAMILY THERAPY

A Guide for Multilateral Systemic Practice in Mental Health and Psychosocial Support

Laurie L. Charlés

Routledge
Taylor & Francis Group

NEW YORK AND LONDON

First published 2021
by Routledge
52 Vanderbilt Avenue, New York, NY 10017

and by Routledge
2 Park Square, Milton Park, Abingdon, Oxon OX14 4RN

Routledge is an imprint of the Taylor & Francis Group, an informa business

Library of Congress Cataloging-in-Publication Data
Names: Charlés, Laurie L., author.
Title: International family therapy : a guide for multilateral systemic practice in mental health and psychosocial support / Laurie L. Charlés.
Description: New York, NY : Routledge, 2021. |
Includes bibliographical references and index.
Identifiers: LCCN 2020038715 (print) | LCCN 2020038716 (ebook) |
ISBN 9780367374983 (hardback) | ISBN 9780367375003 (paperback) |
ISBN 9780429354748 (ebook)
Subjects: LCSH: Family psychotherapy. |
Psychotherapist and patient. | Psychiatry, Transcultural.
Classification: LCC RC488.5 .C4619 2021 (print) |
LCC RC488.5 (ebook) | DDC 616.89/156–dc23
LC record available at https://lccn.loc.gov/2020038715
LC ebook record available at https://lccn.loc.gov/2020038716

ISBN: 978-0-367-37498-3 (hbk)
ISBN: 978-0-367-37500-3 (pbk)
ISBN: 978-0-429-35474-8 (ebk)

Typeset in Joanna
by Newgen Publishing UK

In Memory of my dear friend Muriel Beth Singer (1948–2019).

CONTENTS

A NOTE ABOUT CONFIDENTIALITY

To protect confidentiality, where necessary, I have at times changed or withheld certain of the names and identifying details of projects, countries, or people in the vignettes presented. For the same reason, certain case illustrations and descriptions are composites.

PREFACE

International Family Therapy, which is how I refer both to this book and also to most of the work I am doing these days, came to fruition perhaps as a result of having worked on several books with so many colleagues across the globe in the last few years. I am author or co-editor of several books in the fields of family therapy and qualitative research, most recently: *Family Therapy Supervision in Extraordinary Settings: Illustrations of Systemic Approaches in Everyday Clinical Work*, with Dr. Thorana Nelson (2019), and, with Dr. Gameela Samarasinghe, *Family Systems and Global Humanitarian Mental Health: Approaches in the Field* (2019) and *Family Therapy in Global Humanitarian Contexts: Voices and Issues from the Field* (2016). Gameela and I also worked on a third book, *Psychosocial Innovations in Post-War Sri Lanka* (2015), which we published as an open-access Taos Worldshare Book.

I absolutely loved the process of co-editing books. I did not expect this, and it was a wonderful surprise. One realization from that editing process was this: I felt there was a fairly unknown discourse, a "backstory," if you will, about *Why and How* all those authors from across the globe were doing the family systems work they were doing, at the particular moment they wrote about it. What conditions promoted or inhibited their work? What challenges did they face? How did they meet the challenges? Better yet, how can we make sense of those challenges, from a coherent, systemic view?

This book is a response to my own questions. Perhaps I should have written it before the co-edited books with Gameela and Rana. Yet, I didn't quite see the gap until *after* I'd helped bring those earlier books to fruition. That is how writing works for me, as a form of inquiry, as Laurel Richardson put it. It seemed to me I needed to write a book that was an introduction to those other books. "Ah, yes, here's what I need to say," I thought—after *Extraordinary Supervision* was finally on its way to the publisher. I wrote the proposal for *International Family Therapy* very quickly afterward. I wanted to write a book that brought a systemic lens to looking at all of these global stories, not only clinically, but also from the international plane and within the community of states to which we all belong. I wanted to help to lay the groundwork for family therapists to understand the nature of global work in a useful, multilateral way, while still retaining their systemic sensibility.

My name is Laurie L. Charlés, Ph.D., and I am a systemic family therapy practitioner, clinician, and supervisor. I have worked for multiple international organizations as a family therapy consultant and/or technical officer and subject matter expert. In these roles, I have delivered family therapy training content and provided systemic, clinical supervision support to public mental health professionals living and working in such diverse locations as Guinea during the 2014 Ebola Virus disease epidemic; in post-conflict Sri Lanka; in Syria and Libya; in the Central African Republic; Uzbekistan, and the Maldives to name but a few places. Of note for some of the work I do, I have also lived for extended periods in several countries, including in West Africa, where I was once a Peace Corps Volunteer (Togo, 1999-2001).

I am a trainer and consultant, but also I am a qualitative researcher and a practitioner. I am an AAMFT (American Association for Marriage and Family Therapy) Clinical Fellow and Approved Supervisor, and I have both a doctorate and a master's degree in family therapy. In 2013, I earned a second master's degree, in international relations. Combining two distinct areas of practice, family therapy and international relations, has greatly informed my skill set and consultation practice in international humanitarian relief contexts, in low- and middle-income countries, and with vulnerable populations in conflict-affected states. The hybrid nature of my work these days is a large part of what I will discuss in this book.

Based in Boston, Massachusetts, I am a 2017–2018 Fulbright Global Scholar, and a Lecturer of Family Therapy, with current appointments at the MGH Institute of Health Professions and, recently, at the University of Colombo, Sri Lanka. I've been licensed as a family therapist since 1997, and have held faculty positions at family therapy graduate programs in several U.S. cities and a few countries outside the U.S. I started out in the field doing home-based work and crisis intervention, honing my skills in both my family therapy master's and doctoral programs in San Antonio, Texas, and Ft. Lauderdale, Florida, respectively. In the wake of Covid-19, I am now project lead for a grant award from the U.S. State Department for a Citizen Diplomacy Action Fund (CDAF) Rapid Response to the outbreak. Recently, I was a consultant to a Transitional Justice initiative for an international NGO in Sri Lanka.

I trained under the expert tutelage of folks like Glen Gardner, Monte Bobele, Douglas Flemons, Shelley Green, Ron Chenail, Anne Rambo, and many others. My programs and my professors brought me access to folks like Harry Goolishian, Insoo Kim Berg, and Steve de Shazer, to name just a few. In my doctoral program, I learned the disciplines of writing, of qualitative research, and especially, of research and practice in large-scale crises, which was the focus of my dissertation; a qualitative study of a hostage negotiation (Charlés, 2007).

Today, quite literally as I write this twenty years after I earned my doctorate in family therapy, I find my systemic work remains very much in the field of crisis management and intervention, but from an international, macro perspective, as much as a clinical, micro one. When I am contracted as a subject matter expert, it is because of the skills I bring as a systemically trained clinician, supervisor, and consultant. These skills are so relevant on the international plane.

Currently, I see clients via my virtual office, as tiny as it is global. My work started out in crisis intervention and home-based therapy; it has now transformed to a meta-level of that work, with scholarship and a consultation practice focused on scaling up family therapy practices for host country nationals in fragile, conflict-affected states (FCS). Typically, my role as a consultant is to help enhance public mental health initiatives with vulnerable and at-risk populations in low resource or under-resourced settings across the globe. Many of those settings are FCS; many are low- or middle-income countries—and some of them are both.

Whatever the conditions in a state, there is always a clear line as to why I am there and why I was asked to go. If I take the time to analyze the patterns systemically, I am able to see the shape of the multilateral context that brought me. In this book, I hope to help family therapists understand the international nature of that work. Here, I am writing from first-hand experience and the critical mass of international, global mental health projects where I've been engaged as consultant, trainer, or researcher.

How did I get here? I am often asked a version of this question from up-and-coming family therapists and also well-known, seasoned ones. This book tells that story, to some degree. But the book is not completely about me, even though I am the one typing the lines. I think the book is also a story about the evolution of the field of family therapy, at least from where I sit. It is not a story about the past of family therapy as much as it is a story about the future—the potential of its future I should say, on the international plane. It is a story about family therapy in the midst of the many-sided collaborative process between co-operating states when it comes to families and family focused mental health and psychosocial support.

My story didn't start out so dramatically. Or perhaps I should say, so multilaterally. Over the years, I have been a part of many international projects and initiatives, a number of which I will discuss to some degree in this book. Multiple countries are engaged in these projects, each working as partners to achieve an outcome designed to support best practices for family and community psychosocial health, within state and international norms. Collaborative partnerships between countries make the projects viable, legitimate, and credible. It is a partnership between people (of which I am one), but also, between countries (of which there are many). In this book, I focus on the process one engages in to understand and work from inside a multilateral project, and the things I have learned along the way.

July, 2020
Boston

References

Charlés, L. & Nelson, T. (2019). *Family therapy supervision in extraordinary settings: Illustrations of systemic approaches in everyday clinical work*. Oxford: Routledge.

Charlés, L. & Samarasinghe, G. (2015). *Psychosocial innovation in post-war Sri Lanka* (English version). Chagrin Falls, Ohio: Taos Institute WorldShare Books.

Charlés, L., & Samarasinghe, G. (2016). *Family therapy in global humanitarian contexts: Voices and issues from the field.* New York: Springer.

Charlés, L. & Samarasinghe, G. (2019). *Global humanitarian mental health: approaches in the field.* New York: Springer.

PART I

DESK WORK AND PREPARATION

1

MULTILATERAL FAMILY THERAPY

An Introduction and an Overview

Everything begins with a note of some kind, brief, perhaps an email or a text message. There is a greeting—"Laurie," or, "Dear Dr. Charlés," then a general question, something like: "Are you available? Are you interested?" Next, there will be a specific request, maybe embedded inside a longer description of a project: "We are working to support families in _____. We are focusing on family systems approaches on the issue of _____." The most recent invitations have originated from offices in Vienna, Beirut, and Cairo. Tonight, I leave for Bangkok. I received the email query about Bangkok a month ago. However, I've known about the potential of the Bangkok trip since the project's inception in Vienna 18 months ago. I was a part of the initial design to bring family therapy ideas and practice to this particular multilateral project, designed for implementation across 15 countries in Asia (UNODC, 2020).

The project organized within the United Nations Office in Vienna has undergone various changes and transformations since its inception in June 2018. So, the Bangkok query was not exactly a surprise. But I didn't foresee its arrival on that particular day. Fortunately, I was able to say "Yes." Once I said "Yes," things happened very quickly and also in a kind of strange slow motion. There was so much to do, so many tasks to complete. I'm leaving for the project at 11 p.m. tonight, but I am also teaching a class in a few hours, I have a few potential clients referred to me whom I must now refer out, and I am hoping to get to the gym for a run. Some things will have to wait. The review I'm doing for a journal in the field will have to wait. New clients will have to wait. Working further on this book will have to wait. Many things have to wait. Saying "Yes" also means meticulous planning of my schedule, my time, and my work, mental and physical; it also means being able to let some other things go.

Global Mental Health and Psychosocial Support

The request for my expertise is always quite specific and clear; a contract is involved, for one thing—and that means someone has taken a lot of time to figure out the request. However, essentially, if I had to describe my work in one sentence, I might say: I am hired to travel to a certain place, to train a bunch of folks, themselves from a variety of places, as they work to support families and deliver services in the context of mental health and psychosocial support issues in their country. The requests in these projects are solidly embedded within the realm of global mental health. That is, they are driven by "data about the disparities in mental health and its subsequent access by people across the globe, including disparities between and within states (countries), and between vulnerable groups within states" (Charlés & Bava, 2020). However, they are also focused on mental health and psychosocial support (MHPSS).

In this book, I use the term MHPSS in the way it is described by the Inter-Agency Standing Committee (2010)

> The term "psychosocial" denotes the inter-connection between psychological and social processes and the fact that each continually interacts with and influences the other ... The composite term mental health and psychosocial support (MHPSS) is used to describe any type of local or outside support that aims to protect or promote psychosocial well-being and/or prevent or treat mental disorder.
>
> (IASC, 2010, p. 1)

In my experience, this term is quite useful for family therapists working systemically, particularly because it refers to a broader understanding of health and well-being. The term, for me, fits solidly in many of the clinical and theoretical ideas and issues relevant to systemic theory.

A Note about Systemic Ideas and Family Systems Approaches

The term "systemic" refers to the idea of making sense of behavior within the context in which it occurs (Boscolo, Cecchin, Hoffman & Penn, 1987). Considering the context of families, and behaviors that indicate health or ill health in their lives and in the places they live, is part of what it means to hold a systemic epistemology. Systemic practitioners who focus on families further understand that, in doing so, they are not obligated to an assumption that families only consist of blood relatives. In other words, "family" is not meant only as a referent to blood kin; family in family systems approaches refers to any unit of persons connected to one another.

A family systems approach assumes that the relations between people, whether family or not, have consequences on the well-being of individuals. Thus, a systems approach to psychotherapeutic intervention is focused on the relational pattern of interactions between people. Another way to say this is that systemic clinicians are typically predisposed toward examining *process*. In international work, this is a very useful predisposition indeed. Process is both interaction and language, and these phenomena are always relational. Systems theory, indeed, is evident across many disciplines, and is not solely relegated to family therapy.

Although I am often the lone systemic family therapist in the projects I work in, one mustn't ever assume that just because family therapy professionals are not on the ground across every part of the globe, that systemic family work—often, quite excellent work—is not being done. It is most certainly being done, and quite well in many cases! Although there may not be the regulatory bodies, higher education, or professional associations to represent it, there is generous use of family systems ideas across low- and middle-income countries (LMIC) and in fragile, conflict-affected states (Charlés & Samarasinghe, 2016). While the clinical issues present for those living in these settings are quite similar to what I might see or expect in the U.S., the conditions in the countries are not, and those conditions challenge the work in unexpected ways.

A robust, progressive, multilateral response is required to address these challenges. The field of systemic family therapy, for me, is part of that response. Our field's beginnings are "characterized by multi- and transdisciplinary professionals from across the globe, only some of them focused specifically on clinical work, yet all of them committed to work within the nature of mental process and how it was manifest in societies, in families, and in the nature of their communication with each other" (Charles & Samarasinghe, 2019). It is my hope that this book is a useful guide to international work and, at the same time, mindful of our international origins and our inter-, multi-, and transnational beginnings as a field.

This book addresses a gap in the field: How to prepare family therapists to confidently perform as consultants and trainers from inside the perspective of the international plane, across the global community of states. I use the term *multilateral family therapy* to reflect this perspective. A multilateral approach describes a frame of mind. It is a frame by which to layer one's proficiency as a clinician or trainer within the international system. Multilateral systemic therapy is an approach which allows a professional to work fluently across the international plane, and with others in global mental health.

Working confidently and competently in multilateral projects as a family therapist requires enhancing our understanding of the international system, and how the logic of systemic family therapy and theory is and can be applied across states. It is my hope that this book provides family therapists a guide to the international system, while also outlining the technical skills, range of knowledge, and methods of best practice required to work effectively and intentionally within it. Each of the projects I discuss in this book involves the crossing of country borders, both for me, as a trainer, and also for the participants who are its beneficiary trainees. The streams of funding and the various country/regional partners and collaborators that support the project are yet another international set. However, as the Covid-19 pandemic has shown us, emergencies completely disregard country borders. One can be "deployed" anywhere, at any time, across any part of the globe, when there is an international emergency. Systemic thinkers are particularly needed at such times.

About Multilateral

When I speak of *multilateral* in this book, I am referring to a family therapy training project that is happening across multiple states. In international relations, multilateral refers to several states' robust partnerships in order to meet a common task, or goal. I am also using the term multilateral in this book to conscientously refer to the many-sided, collaborative nature of work on the international plane. Multilateral work is in contrast to efforts that are isolated or singular and, in this way, for me, reflects the systemic nature of so many family therapy ideas. Multilateral work is particularly engaging for family therapists because of its systemic nature; to be multilateral means to engage multiple systems at once and to require systemic collaboration at every level.

As a systemic clinician, one tends to always see the individual while also seeing the larger context. Similarly, today I cannot work in one country without seeing (and conceptualizing) its larger context on the international plane. In the early days of my international work, the projects typically involved only two countries—a bilateral project, if you will. Over the years, that has changed. In concert with the evolution of global mental health, and increased country partnerships specific to scaling up family focused mental health and psychosocial support skills across the globe, most projects I engage in now are clearly multilateral, across multiple state partners, placing me squarely on the global plane as a family therapist.

The second-order shift required to work systemically has its parallel at the international level—one example is the shift from unilateral to multilateral. If you are working systemically with clients, you are already quite literally thinking in a multilateral sort of way. The kind of work I talk about in this book requires that same systemic perspective, but from a "meta" level. Multilateral work is a fine-tuned application of systemic practice, across a transdisciplinary set of ideas, relevant to one's state, and also, to the global community of states.

Multilateral essentially refers to more than one state (country). In the international and global mental health work I am engaged in, this term is very relevant. Multiple country partners often work together, across borders and languages and sets of ideas, in order to achieve a specific goal or mission typically defined as a norm at the international level.

I believe the nature of this work will only increase in the future, and it is with intention that I use it as a subtitle of this book—not to introduce a new model or approach, but rather, as a new way to define what systemic family therapy practice can look like when applied thoughtfully at the international level. Here, I am indebted to the concept of the larger system introduced by Evan Imber-Black (1988) many years ago. Multilateral family therapy, for me, is the larger systems view that occurs from the international plane.

About the Book

Reminiscent of the origins of family therapy, which were not state-specific nor focused in application on any region or geopolitical point on the globe, in this book I focus my lens beyond specific therapy models or particular populations. Combining theoretical tenets of systemic family therapy alongside key concepts and knowledge in international relations, this book is a guide for family therapy practitioners interested in working across states.

Each chapter focuses on specific material that can inform the reader to better understand, appreciate, implement, and critically examine family systems approaches from the perspective of the international plane. This book illustrates a multilateral perspective: A systemic, multi-sided, coherent approach to understanding the international system and working within it. It widens the scope of family systems theory by taking a meta-perspective, a global lens, to the field, considering family therapy intervention and implementation from an international perspective.

The book is divided into three sections. In the first section, "Desk Work and Preparation," I address the critical discourses that inform psychosocial interventions internationally in global mental health, the role of states and state governance in relation to the international system, and the implications of these for the psychosocial well-being of families. The first section includes Chapter 2: "Families, States, and Self-Determination"; Chapter 3, "International Human Rights Law and the Community of States"; Chapter 4, "International Economics and Global Exchanges of Knowledge in Family Therapy"; and Chapter 5, "A Review of Best Practices and International Standards." Chapter 6, "Reflecting on Intervention: Moral Hazards of Multilateral Work," concludes the first section of the book, guiding readers through the international legal norms, standards, and theoretical frameworks used to promote psychosocial support of families and communities across states and state conditions.

The second section, "On the Ground and in the Field," includes chapters with multiple vignettes and illustrations from across the globe, which reflect the trans-, multi-, and interdisciplinary nature and range of clinical work in international and global mental health settings. Through case examples, country scenarios, and personal reflections, I address topics relevant to a multilateral understanding of family systems approaches. The second section is comprised of chapters 7 through 11. Chapter 7 is "'We Don't Think of Our Children as Soldiers: Rehabilitation and Reintegration of Former Child Soldiers in a Region of East Africa." Chapters 8 and 9 tell complementary stories about my work as a Fulbright Global Scholar in two regions of the world, and are named: "Bargaining for the Future: Family Identity and State-Citizen Relational Process in Post-War Kosovo" and "Who Keeps the Peace and Who Makes the Peace? How Family and Community Engagement Is Used to Strengthen Reconciliation and Transitional Justice Mechanisms in Sri Lanka."

Chapter 10 brings together my experiences in the Ebola Virus Disease 2014 Response in Guinea alongside those in Covid-19 in Massachusetts: "Frontline Responses to 'Build Back Better' during Two Public Health Emergencies of International Concern: Guinea during the 2014 Ebola Virus Disease Epidemic and Massachusetts at the Start of the Covid-19 Pandemic." The last chapter of this section, Chapter 11, is "Family Therapy Training in a Multilateral Project: The Transformative Process of a 3D Role-Play in Beirut."

In the third section, "Debrief and Reintegration," I discuss issues of leadership and teamwork in the field, traveling away from and returning home, and re-integrating into one's own community while retaining a global lens and commitment toward one's work and professional development. Chapter 12 is called "Leaving Home: Desk Work and Preparation," and Chapter 13 "Safety and Risk Mitigation: At Home and in the Field." Chapter 14 is "Leading from the Edge and Leading from the Center: Working in International Teams." The final chapter is called "Training the Next Generation of Skilled International Family Therapist." I am grateful to my co-authors in Chapter 15, Florence Lewis, Dorcas Matowe, Melissa Yzaguirre, and Safia Jama, four emerging family therapy practitioners whom I met while volunteering as a Mentor for the AAMFT Minority Fellows Program. I am so appreciative that they were willing to contribute their ideas on what we need to do to train the next generation of skilled, international family therapist.

References

Boscolo, L., Cecchin, G., Hoffman, L. & Penn, P. (1987). *Milan systemic family therapy: Conversations in theory and practice.* New York: Basic.

Charlés, L. & Bava, S. (2020). Family therapy & global mental health: Reflections on professional development and training. In M. Rastogi & R. Singhe (Eds.; K. Wampler, Series Editor), *Handbook of systemic family therapy,* volume IV. New York: Wiley.

Charlés, L., & Samarasinghe, G. (2016). *Family therapy in global humanitarian contexts: Voices and issues from the field.* New York: Springer.

Charlés, L. & Samarasinghe, G. (2019). Introduction. In. L. Charlés & G. Samarasinghe (Eds.) *Global Humanitarian Mental Health: Approaches in the Field.* New York: Springer.

Inter-Agency Standing Committee (IASC) Global Protection Cluster Working Group and IASC Reference Group for Mental Health and Psychosocial Support in Emergency Settings. (2010). *Mental health and psychosocial support in humanitarian emergencies: What should protection programme managers know?* Geneva: Author.

United Nations Office on Drugs and Crime (2020). *Treatment Family: UNODC training materials on elements of family therapy for the treatment of adolescents with drug and other substance use disorders including adolescents in contact with or at risk of contact with the criminal justice system.* Vienna: Author.

2

FAMILIES, STATES, AND SELF-DETERMINATION

The protection of the sovereign state model has increasingly been
supplanted by a human-being oriented approach. ... [and] international
law...must gradually turn to the protection of human beings.

(Tadić appeal chamber ICTY, cited by Cryer,
Friman, Robinson, & Wilmshurst, 2007)

In Manila, my family therapy classes consisted of students from half a
dozen countries across Asia—East Timor, Indonesia, Vietnam, Laos,
Cambodia, and of course, the Philippines (Charlés, 2007). They had
in common: (1) Citizenship in the region of neighboring countries;
(2) A specific interest to travel to Manila to be trained as psychologists;
and, most significantly; (3) The intention to be trained in English.

At the time, I thought of my mixture of international students as fascinating. However, I saw this primarily through a lens of cultural diversity. Rich as this lens is, it didn't give me a robust way to analyze how
I understood the context of the region's particular languages, religions,

and histories. Nor did I have a framework to think about each state's governance, or the relational process of trade between the states in the region. I did know quite a bit about some of the countries. However, I had never considered them in relationship to each other, which was essentially a key part of the students' identities represented in my classroom. I was traveling with a standard playbook of questions—albeit important ones—about the cultures of individual families, rather than *a set of questions about the cultures of nations.*

In this chapter, I want to talk about governance, about the relationship a state has with its citizens, and how all of it can be useful to consider when one is working multilaterally.

Families Are Embedded in a Multi-Country Relational Process

Today, I can see quite clearly that I didn't really have a method for understanding in any meaningful way the students' *multi-country relational process with each other.* I could certainly, and expertly, even, understand their cultural contexts as individuals. However, I had no framework to think about how to take this data to a meta-level, no way by which to understand them as *a system of regional citizens.* Yet the classes went well, and I had a wonderful experience in Manila. However, today, I have a much broader intersectional lens with which to view the work I was doing in that part of Asia.

There is no place I have worked as a family therapist where families and family ties are not valued as the highest form of group cohesion in a society. Family, as metaphor, as phenomenon, speaks to the past, to the present, and of course, the future. Family speaks to one's identity, to one's sense of belonging, and to both progress as well as the legacies of history. Families are important in ways that people do not question or protest. Although of course people may question what a family *is*—its definition is always at the same time something resistant to definition—that doesn't prevent people from trying to define it, or stake a claim on what it means or what its values should represent.

I've yet to witness citizens in any country or community question the value of family, of the role it plays, and of its importance in life. In this way, family, as an institution, stands apart. Yet, family does not exist in a vacuum. It is immutable, perhaps, but it is never without its larger influences, its *larger system*, as Evan Imber-Black put it many years ago. Larger systems, like families, are dynamic and in a constant state of change. One of the most important of these influences is the nation-state.

States Are Systems

States are not people nor are they are "family," but they are most certainly systems (Charlés, 2015). The system and nature of governance in a state can be helpful in understanding how a family sees itself and how it negotiates its identity. Families always see themselves in unique, critical ways. States are no different. It is the relationship between them, between state and family, that is key to understanding so many *other* things. Fluency needed to work effectively on the international plane includes broader conceptualizations of systems to include states and governance, which can help us understand, analyze, and promote the social determinants of health.

I once had a professor in Cairo tell me, "States are juridical abstractions; however, to their citizens, they are real enough." A critical way to understand how a state sees its citizens and how citizens see the state, and how they work in relation to each other, is to take a look at the state's form of governance. What constitutes the relationship between the state (government) and its citizenry? What is or has been its trajectory? What is its evolution? My questions are certainly not new. Indeed, "The relationship between the individual and the political community has been explored everywhere through the ages. However, there are some experiences that have given rise to different models of citizenship: Above all, the Greek participatory notion and the Roman status structure" (Parolin, 2009, p. 19).

In discussing the relationship between a state and its citizenry in this chapter, I am borrowing from the work of Gianluca Parolin (2009), and his book, *Citizenship in the Arab World: Kin, Religion, and Nation-State*. Analyzing the nature and history of the very idea of "citizenship," and drawing robustly on original Arabic sources, Parolin writes that

> In the quest for a core notion of citizenship, Aristotle's definition can be viewed as a starting point; both Western and Eastern scholars have used the Aristotelian definition as a basis, at times to refine it,

sometimes to extend its scope or even to contest it. Investigating the social and political nature of man was the innermost and earliest level of inquiry into the texture of human relations in ancient philosophy. In this context, Aristotle was the first to bring man to the centre of the stage and to argue that his distinctive character was his being "political"; human beings, unlike animals or gods, are political by nature.

(p. 17)

Parolin notes that Aristotle's axiom influenced generations of intellectuals both in the East and in the West. In his analysis, Parolin notes that "[t]he contrasting paradigms of citizenship in classical Greece and republican Rome affected the development of citizenship theories in the West more than in the Eastern world" (Parolin, 2009, p. 19), and also, that "[i]n the West, the concept of the individual started surfacing in the late Middle Ages against the backdrop of an orderly socio-political system characterised by the presence of local and universal powers" (p. 21).

Looking more broadly across global contexts and notions of citizenship, Parolin (2009) finds that the "Latin and the Arab worlds followed different paths, even if they both drew on Greek philosophy, which supplied categories and terminology later employed to deal with various new issues" (p. 21). Parolin continues,

In spite of the differences between Latin-Christian and Arab-Islamic results, the themes, the processes and somehow even the terms are analogous; this has always facilitated the comparison between the systems, but at the same time it has made the (op)positions look more extreme. It is hard to determine when the two paths drifted apart; up to the 13th century, anecdotes of Frederick II commending the Islamic caliphal system out of scorn for papal authority (Kantorowicz 1931) prove that a close comparison was still feasible, even if the two worlds were already significantly far removed from each other.

(p. 21)

Citizenship Is a Relational Process

I did not expect to be quoting, or quoting someone else who was quoting, Aristotle and Plato in a book about family therapy. I do so here primarily as a way to organize my discussion about citizenship as a form of identity. Citizenship implies a legal relationship a person has with their government; however, I use the term more broadly here, to refer to the *relational process* a person has with their sovereign state(s). At the same time, I absolutely agree that "citizenship" is a relational process that goes *beyond* any specific country. Indeed, "in a globalized world, citizenship is no longer a matter under exclusive control of sovereign states" (Baubock, 2009, p. 11).

As Aristotle knew (read on) family is also the core relationship an individual has with an external set of "others." The state, then, and its relationship with its people, that is, families, is key to unfolding our discussion of international and global meanings around these two social units.

Perhaps we think of states mostly in terms of their borders, or their currencies, or their wars. We may think of a state in terms of its leadership, or how it handles emergencies such as a pandemic. We may think about it in terms of its geography—its beautiful locations or its natural resources. Our distinctions are based on our experiences and values, certainly, but also, perhaps, from epistemological ideals within our unique disciplines. Perhaps, we may not even think of a state at all. Indeed, the state most certainly is a juridical abstraction. Yet, it has a deep influence on family life. Parolin (2009) found the same in his historical analysis, illustrated in a discussion and comparison between Aristotle and Plato:

> According to Aristotle, man (a`nthrō̄ pos) leads by nature a social life, whose typical form is the polis. Hence, the citizen (poli`f es)—namely, the man who actively takes part in public life by exercising political and judicial functions—is the human being who fulfills his humanity. Before being a member of the polis, however, man is a member of his family (oiki`a), a minor social unit that Plato looked at as a hindrance to his perfect city, whereas Aristotle considered it a "natural" form of membership.
>
> (p. 18)

Integrating a fundamental understanding of both family and state is essential to a multilateral view. It can be helpful for international systemic family therapists to learn something about the institution of a state. It is as important as the notion of systemic family therapists, who want professionals in the related social sciences to learn something of the science, with regard to the institution of family, and especially, the psychosocial interventions that are designed to support it.

A State Is Its Relationship with Its Citizens

Since the Westphalian era, the development of sovereignty within borders creating "states," and the "five hundred years that numerous scholars mark the divide between modern and premodern times" (Kennedy, 1987, p. 3), countries have been categorized in a number of different ways. Economics and trade, political science, and international relations scholars would each view a state, and, in turn, its state actors, or the agents of a state, in a particular way. States are not people. Yet, they act through agents, who are most certainly people. Thus, the use of the term state actors (and its complement, non-state actors) is a critical distinction.

Understanding the role of governance in a state means having some recognition of what constitutes a state in the first place. We may be accustomed to asking clients, "Can you tell me a little bit about your family?" But, how do we question a "state"? How do we ask about its identity? States are not people, but it is people who make the state work; it is people who are influenced by the "international or national macro-developments, which then, in turn influence national-level legal and policy outcomes" (Goodman & Jinks, 2013, p. 13).

Goodman and Jinks (2013) posit, in their book, *Socializing States*, that in addition to materially inducing states or persuading states to act a certain way, the international system changes state behavior through a process of *acculturation*. They explain, "By acculturation, we mean the general process by which actors adopt the beliefs and behavioral patterns of the surrounding culture" (p. 4).

In proposing the idea of states' acculturation and assimilation as social and relational processes, these authors suggest that the outcomes are only partially derived through law and legal institutions. They posit that states, indeed, are socialized toward a field of action, "by way of multiple, discrete mechanisms including acculturation. These mechanisms, in turn, operate through various 'microprocesses' at the individual level" (Goodman & Jinks, 2013, p. 9). As they explain further, those at the individual level include "government officials, policy advisors, members of the national and local media, issue-specific activists, and even ordinary citizens" (Goodman & Jinks, 2013, p. 13).

Charles Tilly on State-Making, War-Making, Protection, and Extraction

The sociologist Charles Tilly (1990) distinctly clarified the activities of the European state as *State-making, War-making, Protection*, and, as a means to achieve these three, *Extraction*. State-making activities focus on activities "attacking and checking competitors and challengers within the territory claimed by the state." War-making activities focus on "attacking rivals outside the territory already claimed by the state." Protection activities focus on "attacking and checking rivals of the rulers' principal allies, whether inside or outside the state's claimed territory." Extraction activities refer to "drawing from the subject population the means of state-making, war-making, and protection" (p. 96).

As European states moved from indirect to direct rule, and from insubordination to assimilation, they also promoted the homogenization of their populations in order to break down their segmentation. A significant method by which this was done was by imposing common languages, religions, currencies, and legal systems. States also attempted to achieve this by "promoting the construction of connected systems of trade, transportation, and communication" (Tilly, 1990, p. 100).

According to Tilly (1990), while the four activities of state-making, war-making, protection, and extraction are indispensable to the state, it is three other areas that are increasingly relevant. These areas include: (1) Adjudication, or "authoritative settlement of disputes among members of the subject population"; (2) distribution, or "intervention in the allocation of goods among members of the district population"; and (3) production, or "control of the creation and transformation of goods and services by members of the subject population" (p. 96–97).

These three latter activities—adjudication, distribution, and production— have profound implications for the interests of the general population, because of the very real effects they have on people's everyday lives. When citizens resist these real effects, they may do so in the form of making new claims on the state (Tilly, 1990). This transformation is not achieved without struggle, however. Yet for Tilly (1990), it is in the struggle that democracy is developed.

It is also in the process of this struggle, this bargaining with the state, that citizens created their individual and collective rights as subjects of the state, and parties identified the obligations of the state to its citizens. The bargaining process, very much a relational, systemic one, created rights for citizens. As Tilly (1990) put it, this process "*recognized enforceable claims of states with respect to their citizens.*" Tilly summarizes this bargaining process in the statement: "The core of what we now call 'citizenship' indeed, consists of multiple bargains hammered out by rulers and ruled in the course of their struggles over the means of state action, especially the making of war" (p. 101–102). Ironically, "the struggle over the means of war produced state structures that no one had planned to create, or even particularly desired" (Tilly, 1990, p. 117).

Citizens and States: Consolidating for the Future

Tilly (1990) has outlined how coercive activities formed the core of European states for a thousand years. However, as state's activities grew beyond a coercive core and militarization, citizens' claims also grew, to include a wide range of activities in the areas of protection, adjudication, production, and distribution. All along this continuum, citizens' bargaining over the state's extractive claims produced rights, privileges, and protective institutions that did not previously exist.

Additionally, war imposed upon the state the necessity to obtain resources. Those resources came from the activity of extraction that the state obtained from its population. To obtain an efficient extraction, the state created administrative structures to monitor and control the population, with the aid of its coercive power. Bargaining processes between the state and its citizens further moved the state to such actions as creating a judiciary system to protect those relations.

Each and all of these processes develop state capacity, on the one hand, and on the other, they form the basis for citizenship. When citizenship attains a certain degree, it has the capacity to achieve democracy. Democracy can take many forms and exist in states with autocratic, democratic, or plutocratic governments. Democracy, however, is more than a descriptive label—its authenticity and authority are credible only when supported by particular conditions. These conditions, among other things, help to measure whether or not a democracy is "consolidated" or "unconsolidated."

According to Linz & Stepan (1996), a consolidated democracy is one that is characterized by three key dimensions:

1. Behavioral: No significant national, social, economic, political, or institutional actors spend significant resources attempting to achieve their objectives by creating a nondemocratic regime or by seceding from the state;
2. Attitudinal: When a strong majority of public opinion, even in the midst of major economic problems and deep dissatisfaction with incumbents, holds the belief that democratic procedures and institutions are the most appropriate way to govern collective life, and when support for alternatives is quite small or more-or-less isolated from pro-democratic forces; and
3. Constitutional: When governmental and nongovernmental forces alike become subject to, and habituated to, the resolution of conflict within the bounds of the specific laws, procedures, and institutions sanctioned by the new democratic process. (p. 15–16)

The institutional changes associated with democratization are reinforced by the key tenets that Tilly (2002) describes as key aspects of democratization: *the transformation and approach toward public politics; handling the issue of inequality; and addressing issues of public trust.* Institutional capacity and transparency, encouragement of trust-bearing networks, and addressing systems of equality are key to democratization. Emerging consolidated democracies cement their gains by "looking beyond their borders" to enhance their own processes by partnering with like-minded nations. Globalization has played a significant role in cementing and reinforcing consolidated democracies. Essentially, consolidated (or consolidating) democracies were institutionally better positioned to economically adapt to globalization and thus more quickly benefited from its growth and spread.

Unconsolidated Democracies—The Effect of Internal Conflicts and Weak Institutions

Why is there no (or slow) movement toward consolidated democracy in some parts of the world? The answer to why is multi-fold: First, the core institutional capacity of many nations is weak. Second, key tenets of what helps democracies endure and mature are missing. Third, while economic performance is a clear and critical variable in helping countries democratically mature, we often see that autocratic regimes place so much emphasis on economic development that other aspects of democratization are left unaddressed.

Further, in many nations, the will of leaders to reform is significantly lacking. That is, there is little or no interest in bargaining with the people, in the way that Tilly outlined so coherently. This shortcoming is manifest in the failure of leaders to address the very negative impact that income inequality has on the political dynamic. Inequality is a real threat to democracy development, because it has the potential to reproduce itself as divisions within the public political sphere (Tilly, 2002, p. 199).

State Failure

State failure is synonymous with a lack of empirical sovereignty in all or parts of a territory for which a state can claim (often successfully) juridical sovereignty. State failure is a process along a continuum, illustrating various stages of weakness, and judged on the basis of performance criteria. State failure can mean that a nation can no longer be treated as a sovereign state. For example, it may have lost the ability to secure its military; have pockets of insurgency in contested zones; lack sophisticated command and control systems of its nuclear arsenal, making it more vulnerable to attack; or lacking in a coherent grand strategy or military doctrine (rendering it vulnerable and incapable).

State failure is not only about control of an entire state but also of parts of a given state's territory. A failed state can mean a lack of control of state infrastructure, creating a zone or region of volatility in what may already be a contested area. The geographic proximity between a failed state and other, nearby states—whether friend or foe—puts everyone at great risk, potentially affecting a wide range of countries in the region, given the interdependence among economic, diplomatic, and military ties. This can create zones of insurgency and conflict, involving identity groups divided by state borders, yet who support each other in various struggles for rights, development, and a share in or control over local resources.

Human Security and Development as Freedom (Amartya Sen)

One important aspect of understanding families, states, and their ongoing development and progress is the notion of security. Karns and Mingst (2008) provide a useful definition of the changing definition of this term:

> Traditionally, security in the Westphalian sense meant *state* security— the security of borders, control over population, and freedom from interference in the government's sovereignty over internal affairs. With the body of internationally recognized human rights norms steadily expanding in the second half of the twentieth century, the balance between the rights of sovereign states and the rights of people began to shift. Increasingly, it was argued that *human* security should take precedence over security of governments or states.
>
> (p. 293)

While states are often focused, as noted above, on security with regard to militarisation, this element of state-making has been criticized as insufficient with regard to a state's responsibility to its citizens beyond their protection during war. It is in this way that the idea of human security finds its relevance in the field of mental health and psychosocial support, and also, of course, in international family therapy. "Human security recognises the widespread and cross-cutting issues that threaten the viability of not only states but the people and communities that comprise them. Its point of departure is grounded in the fact the traditional concept of security goes beyond that of threats to people, communities and states posed by crime, war or terrorism" (Young, 2019, pp. 80–81).

As Young further explains,

> [T]he human security approach was introduced in 1994 via the global Human Development Report (HDR) where the focus was on

the two (2) main components of human security: "freedom from fear" and "freedom from want." These were inspired by the Universal Declaration of Human Rights. . . . In the 1990s, the freedom "to live in dignity" was also added with the increasing focus on not just identifying threats but analysing the root causes underpinning these threats.

(Young, 2019, pp. 80–81)

The notion of freedom as development, and development as freedom (Sen, 1999) is another more recent addition to the scholarship and world of ideas relevant to our understanding of the interdependency between families, states, and self-determination. Our ability to work multilaterally as a family therapist requires us to be sensitive to the changing nature of state governance, from within the international system. It is deeply enhanced with a fundamental set of concepts at hand to look systemically at state–citizen relations. This harmony of knowledge must be integrated with current events and inclusive of multiple, complex factors that are usually considered in isolation. Systemic theorists are expert at this type of analysis. However, to conduct it, we will be better informed by including data on a country's diplomacy, the nature of its "war-making," including its military apparatus, its economic policies and efforts at extraction, and, of course, its civil society—the trust-bearing networks of identity and the nature of inequality inside it. Families remain a key component of such analysis.

References

Baubock, R. (2009). Preface. In Parolin, G. (2009). *Citizenship in the Arab world: Kin, religion and nation-state.* Amsterdam: Amsterdam University Press.

Charlés, L. (2007). Cultural competency as a relational process: Scenes from a family therapy context in the Philippines. *Qualitative Inquiry, 13* (8), 1160–1176.

Charlés, L. L. (2015). Scaling up family therapy in fragile, conflict-affected states. *Family Process, 54,* 545–558. doi:10.1111/famp.12107

Cryer, R., Friman, H., Robinson, D., & Wilmshurst, E. (2007). *An introduction to international criminal law and procedure.* New York: Cambridge University Press.

Goodman, R., & Jinks, D. (2013). *Socializing states: Promoting human rights through international law*. New York: Oxford University Press.

Kantorowicz, E. (1931). *Kaiser Friedrich der Zweite*. London: Constable.

Karns, M. P., & Mingst, K. A. (2010). *International organizations: The politics and processes of global governance*. Boulder, CO: Lynne Rienner.

Kennedy, P. (1987). *The rise and fall of the great powers: Economic change and military conflict from 1500 to 2000*. New York: Random House.

Linz, J., & Stepan, A. (1996). Toward consolidated democracies. *Journal of Democracy, 7* (2), 14–33.

Parolin, G. (2009). *Citizenship in the Arab world: Kin, religion and nation-state*. Amsterdam: Amsterdam University Press.

Sen, A. (1999). *Development as freedom*. New York: Knopf.

Tilly, C. 1990. *Coercion, capital, and European states, A.D. 990–1990*. Oxford, U.K.: Blackwell.

Tilly, C. (2002). *Stories, identities, and political change*. New York: Rowman & Littlefield.

Young, S. (2019). Between family and foreign policy: A gendered approach to understanding the impact of foreign policy failure on human security in the SIDS of the Caribbean. In L. L. Charles & G Samarasinghe (Eds.), *Family systems and global humanitarian mental health*. New York: Springer.

3

INTERNATIONAL HUMAN RIGHTS LAW AND THE COMMUNITY OF STATES

"Ubi Societas, Ibi Jus" — "Wherever there is a society, there is law"

If I had to pick the moments of my life in which my family therapy world shifted toward a global arc, one of those would be at the University of Massachusetts in Boston, where I was teaching family therapy graduate students in 2008. At the time, I was also working as a consultant for a local National Consortium of Torture Treatment Programs (NCTTP) site, providing clinical supervision and MHPSS (Mental Health and Psychosocial Support) program support. The site's administration had been going through many changes. A new executive team at the site brought a kind of upheaval; within a few weeks of my arrival, the only two clinicians who worked at the site resigned. I remained on board as the consultant supervisor, but there were no longer any therapists to supervise. The clients of the program, all refugees and survivors of torture displaced to the U.S., had no MPHSS staff to support them.

At around the same time, I had embarked on a qualitative research training project for my students, who had expressed interest in working with refugees in Boston. In the project, which was later published as an article in the Journal of Marital and Family Therapy (Charlés, Moebus, Beechinor, Pearce & Putney, 2014), I had integrated qualitative research methodology with critical ethnography and international human rights law content to help promote the students' capacity to work with war-affected populations. I later went on to do several versions of this project in fragile, conflict-affected states—finding it to be very transportable and useful.

Fortuitously, that qualitative training project became key to resolving my dilemma at the NCTTP site. The students who I had recruited as participants in the qualitative project had had to complete a 44-hour curriculum, which included essentials of qualitative research methods, including how to conduct focus groups. This was to prepare them to conduct interviews at the project's culmination: Two days of focus group discussions with Iraqi, Cambodian, and Bhutanese refugees living in Greater Boston. The training was meant to prepare them to lead the focus groups. However, it seemed also to be perfect as an orientation for the students to deliver clinical services at the NCTTP site as interns.

Looking back, I can see a clear thread tying together what at times have felt like many disparate, even random, interests I've had throughout my career. Back then, I had no idea that those projects would turn out the way they did, nor that they would be so complementary. The connections seem clear in hindsight, but at the time, they felt somewhat peripatetic. I had moved to Boston from Florida to take the faculty teaching job I had been offered. I had wanted to live and work in a place where I could continue doing work with survivors of atrocities, but I had no idea beforehand exactly how I would do that. I only knew I wanted to continue some version of the work I'd started as a pro bono home-based clinician at a different NCTTP program on Florida's west coast.

The Florida work had begun in yet another unexpected way. With some of my dear friends and colleagues from Nova Southeastern University, I had presented at a unique professional conference in Washington, D.C. (Charlés & Singer, 2005). I had been so inspired there, by my colleagues' work certainly, but also by the work of people focusing on families who had experienced atrocities. In fact, this was a common theme at the conference. I was so energized by all of it. When I came home, I called the torture treatment program outside Tampa and offered my skills as a volunteer, home-based clinician.

I became good friends with my new colleagues in Tampa; we worked on other projects (Charlés & Blair, 2006) together and have stayed in touch through the years. I went on to do many other related projects, including training torture treatment providers to conduct qualitative interviews with beneficiaries; supervising clinicians working in contexts of families' forced displacement; conducting rapid needs assessments in conflict-affected states; and also, volunteering as an asylum evaluator—something I still do today. The work has been so rewarding.

However, there are also, often, seemingly insurmountable obstacles. Early in my time in Boston, one of the other organizations I worked with had had a client who had needed family therapy clinical services in Arabic. However, the organization had had no one to refer this client to; no one in their network spoke fluent Arabic. Today that is not an issue; however, at the time, such resources were scarce. At that time, I did have a student who was fluent in Arabic, having grown up in Arabic speaking countries her entire life. She was bright, lively, and intellectually and emotionally mature enough to do the work. However, she was newly enrolled in our program. She did not have any form of clinical experience.

I had plenty of proficient, sharp students I was supervising, many of whom wanted to work with torture survivors. Yet, none of them spoke Arabic; nor did they have any understanding of torture or its clinical sequelae. I couldn't do anything about the lack of access to Arabic, not in the short run. However, I realized perhaps I could do something fairly rapidly about the students' lack of understanding about torture. Indeed, that was one of the precipitating events for me to devise the qualitative research training project in the first place.

In my career, I have found that the feeling of frustration, especially if intense and persistent, often leads me to some form of professional and personal innovation and creativity. It will guide me if I let it. In this case, I found part of what would become a large part of my professional voice by doing something very routine for family therapy faculty everywhere: I wrote up a grant proposal and asked my department for research money.

After securing funding and getting Institutional Review Board (IRB) approval, I developed and implemented that curriculum for my students (Charlés, et al, 2014). This was the curriculum that became so critical for them at the NCTTP site.

The curriculum I had created for my Boston students focused on qualitative research inquiry with families from conflict-affected countries who were forcibly displaced survivors of torture. The students were proficient clinical trainees and they took to the qualitative methodology practice exercises like fish to water. However, the content in qualitative research turned out to be only one part of what they needed to know. The curriculum quickly evolved to include material about what the students seemed most unfamiliar with and most confused by: The historical and contemporary national and international human rights issues that created refugees and torture survivors in the first place. I found myself creating modules that could help address students' brilliant questions, which included things like: *What is statelessness? What is the difference between a refugee, asylum seeker or IDP? What is torture? What is political persecution? What is a fragile state and why might this be important to know? What does mental health look like in conflict-affected countries?*

The students' questions went beyond culture, beyond identity, and beyond language. They are questions that are addressed across many disciplines, including but not limited to international human rights law. I had had many of these questions, too. But I also had answers—and, better yet, I had material sources. I had just returned from a three-month deployment in the Central African Republic as a mental health officer for an international organization. Serendipitously (again), I had many pieces of useful content and media at my disposal to share with them about the role of international human rights law in mental health and psychosocial support.

In Boston, my trainees had not been living in a state of ongoing, armed conflict; none of them had had direct experience with atrocities such as Crimes against Humanity. However, the research project's refugee participants (and also, as it turned out, the students' future clients) most certainly did. I decided that I could scale up the students' knowledge, potentially enhancing the skill set they could use when encountering CaH—which they were certainly likely to do if they stayed in Boston.

CaH, the acronym for Crimes against Humanity, is summarized as "the commission of certain inhumane acts, such as murder, torture, rape, sexual slavery, persecution and other inhuman acts" as part of a "widespread or systematic attack directed against a civilian population" (Cryer, Friman, Robinson & Wilmshurst , 2007, p. 230). The full definition from the Rome Statute of the International Criminal Court can be found at United Nations. These crimes are seen by the international community as a violation of rights against individuals, of rights that are universal, that is, owed to everyone. Thus, they are seen as a violation of rights against society. According to Bassiouni (2011),

> The origin of the term 'crimes against humanity' can be traced back to a joint declaration of the French, British and Russian governments, dated May 24, 1915, that addressed the World War I era crimes committed by the Ottoman Empire against its Armenian population.
>
> (ibid., p. 1)

While each of the different backgrounds of my students in Boston meant that they would be heightening their awareness and sensitivity (Laszloffy & Habekost, 2010) to Crimes against Humanity (CaH) in different ways, I found I could address that with a broader set of questions. In other words, through an understanding and sensitivity to international human rights law, I could heighten their cultural awareness and sensitivity from another angle, a different point of perspective.

This was a new intersection for me, and maybe, perhaps for good reason. According to Bassiouni (2011, p. 5), "International law, which is the product of state decision-making, has largely ignored social and behavioral sciences to be less encumbered by scientific findings when state interests are at stake." Interestingly, Bassiouni (ibid.) also noted that the

> Political, social, and behavioral sciences have each developed techniques and methodologies for determining the causes of violent manifestations, as well as some measurements to assess their outcomes. But these disciplines are insufficiently developed to influence policy making in connection with the prevention or limiting of violent interaction, whether at the interstate or domestic levels.

Public International Law

Public international law, from which international human rights law is derived, is a set of rules between states. It is made for states, by states, and serves both the purpose of regulating state behavior, as well as protecting the rights of individuals. States are the primary subjects of international law; however, human rights conventions confer rights on individuals. International criminal justice is thus different from 'ordinary' prosecution and criminal justice at the domestic level. Schabas (2012), in his discussion of atrocity crimes, helps to make the difference quite clear:

> In one sense, international crimes such as genocide resemble ordinary crimes such as murder. But they also require additional elements of *context, intent, scale,* or *gravity.* While so-called ordinary crimes are the work of social deviants, international crimes usually require some degree of involvement by the state, that is, by the very organ whose purpose it is to protect society.
>
> (ibid., p. 22)

Another way to think about this: "Individuals have intent. States have policies" (ibid., p. 147).

States are sovereign and independent, and, within their own boundaries, considered "equal" to one another. However, the ideology of public international law assumes it is possible to grow out of one's national interests, and to be bound by a shared duty that is concerned with the conduct between states and with norms and values that transcend any one state or statehood. It is the relationship between states that makes international law and justice of a different order. As Schabas put it:

> In addressing all of these dimensions of international justice, there is a tendency towards mechanistic transposition to the international level of ideas and principles that have been derived from national criminal justice. But international justice is different. Its political dimensions are inescapable. Its objectives necessarily involve goals related to conflict prevention and conflict resolution. ... If it can work effectively,

there is the potential to contribute to addressing some of the great problems of our time.

(ibid., p. 22–23)

International law can be seen as a way to understand those values that are protected by international law's prohibitions. International crimes are considered to be those crimes which are of great concern to the international community as a whole (Cryer et al, 2007). Breaches of international law occur when there is a violation of an international obligation applicable to and binding on the state.

At this point in the chapter I think it would be very appropriate for a reader to wonder: What is the relevance of public international law (PIL), and why, as a family therapist, would I want know anything about it? There are so many reasons! But one of the most compelling things I have found about PIL is its consistency with the values of social justice many western-trained systemic clinicians aspire to, which are termed very differently from country to country, yet make a kind of very coherent sense when viewed from the international plane. Rather than imposing my idea of what social justice is in a community of which I am not a member nor cultural insider, and rather than using terminology that is so contextually derived, I have found PIL can help me draw on a broader understanding of injustice.

In many countries where I've worked, it is dangerous to use a term like "social justice." One might think that terms from public international law are equally risky. Yet, I've discovered my colleagues in low- and middle-income countries or fragile, conflict-affected states, are actually more likely to know and quote the treaties and conventions that are relevant and binding to their country's actions or inactions about a particular issue (Charlés, 2015). They quote statutes or definitions verbatim; they often know exactly what is happening with regard to their state's behavior specific to an international norm. Using the exact language from a treaty is sometimes safer to use than a more general phrase; "social justice," can be mistaken as an export "from the west." I think my colleagues in LMICs and FCS know more about treaties and conventions because they directly relate to their lives. Whatever the reason, it has been incredibly powerful for me to learn this.

The way a state sees itself and its relationship to other states as well as on the international plane has real implications for the families who live there. It has implications for how citizens of other states see them. Sometimes, depending perhaps on the bargain that is struck (or not) between a state and its citizens, that type of information is front and center. In other states, it can be less evident, somewhat hidden from view.

Public international law is always present; it affects our lives in innumerable ways. Further, international human rights law informs the norms by which most systemic family therapists aspire to practice. As Anthony Cassese put it: "[I]n the current framework of the international community, three sets of values underpin the overarching system of interstate relations: peace, human rights, and self-determination" (1999).

The Doctrine of the Sources

Typically, in a legal system, there are three institutions: Legislative, executive, and judiciary. However, in public international law, this system does not exist in the traditional way we know and understand law. International law does not fit the model of domestic law, with a parliament, a president, ministers or a legislative body. However, that public international law does not look like domestic law does not mean it is not law. Public international law is a legal system; it exists on a different level than domestic systems.

So, how is public international law made? Public international law is made through what is called the *doctrine of the sources* of international law—a set of agreed upon processes, techniques and methods, which specify how law is made. These include: Treaties (also known as Conventions), Customs or Customary Law, and General Principles. The doctrine of the sources of international law are defined in Article 38 of the International Court of Justice, established by the Charter of the United Nations as the principal judicial organ of the United Nations (1945).[1]

The Charter of the United Nations is a treaty.

[T]hat it happens to be one of the most-widely ratified treaties in the history of international relations does signal the concomitant fact that it is not an ordinary treaty ... the members of the United Nations, by the fact of their membership, have not merely become parties to a treaty but members of a *community*.

(Chesterman, Franck & Malone, 2008, p. 4–5)

This community, as constituted by the states' agreement to the treaty, refers to the social contract between them, not as persons, but as states. The treaty is inherently normative, but this is only part of its role as an instrument. The UN Charter, or treaty, constitutes the international community, whereby states "agree to enter a continuing relationship … [that] constitutes an ongoing process of interaction and not simply a substantive set of rules" (ibid., p. 5).

Pacta Sunt Servanda

A treaty is best understood as a source of obligation and the only rule of law in the matter is the basic principle *pacta sunt servanda*: "Every treaty is binding upon the parties to it and must be performed by them in good faith" (Article 26, VCLT).[2]

Treaties are often preferable as a source of law because they are written documents, with signatories, which can make them seem more real— certainly, more tangible. While a treaty has clear state obligations, it may also contain reservations. Reservations are that part of the treaty to which a state does not agree, even if they are signatory to the treaty. Treaties sometimes have enforcement provisions, and typically they are more enforceable than customary law.

Customary Law

Norms also emerge through the practice of states, or, through a state's customs. This results in what is called customary law and it is binding on a state. Customary law is one of the more fascinating components of public international law for me, as it seems to speak so directly to the less tangible, but still very real, data of context, relationship, and interaction. While the data of customary law appears quite ambiguous (like trying to explain what "context" is, for example), it can become clearer with rigorous examination.

There are four elements which demonstrate that customary law exists: *Duration of practice; repetition of practice; continuity of practice; generality of practice* (referring to an adequate number of states also doing it). You can find customary law in a state's diplomatic correspondence and its press releases; in its legislation and court decisions; in its participation in international organizations or in treaties.

Interestingly, a treaty can embody already established rules of customary law, thus becoming a declaration of existing rules. Customary law requires two conditions: "general practice" and a "conviction that something is dictated by a *legal norm*." Norms are critical in international law, as there is no "international government"—what then emerges as a set of norms is fluid, contextual, yet also, very much based in the "data" of practice of a state, that is, what it *does*.

It can be useful here to discuss briefly the concept of international norms, sometimes referred to as "soft law." Family therapists working from a systemic epistemology certainly understand the concept of norms, as applied to family life and assessment, that is, what a family system does and how it is organized. In international work, when focused on the community of states, scholars also recognize the importance of norms, and examine how they vary in strength, how they "emerge," and, of course, how and whether or not they are violated (Karns & Mingst, 2010).

It is worth noting here that international norms are also constitutive of the action of both states *and* non-state actors. "Non-state actors are not sovereign and do not have the same kind of power resources as states" (ibid., p. 221). Yet, they can play key roles in global governance. Non-state actors may include "non-governmental organizations (NGO)s or international NGOs, transnational networks and coalitions, experts and epistemic communities, foundations and multinational corporations, multi stakeholder actors, and social movements" (ibid., p. 222).

General Principles

General principles of law are principles that can be theoretically found in all dominant legal traditions, not necessarily just traditions in the global north. They include but are not limited to: Good faith; that one shall not be a judge in your own case; the finality of judgments; freedom of the seas; freedom of outer space; good neighborliness; that treaties must be respected; that there is sovereign equality. There is no book or catalogue or place that lists general principles. In the absence of customary law and treaty law, general principle can fill in gaps. However, while the International Court of Justice (ICJ) has never decided a case solely on General Principles, they are often included alongside customary law or treaty law.

As do many disciplines, certainly inclusive of family therapy, international law, as a field, has its hubris as well as its narratives of deliverance (Kennedy, 1985; Kennedy, 2004; Korhonen, 1996; Koskenniemi, 2003; Koskenniemi, 2009; Skouteris, 2009b). It has a post-modern, social constructionist turn. Like systemic family therapy, it is both practice oriented and at the same time, a self-reflexive critique of its orientation and practice. Its origins and its contemporary scholarship are broad and deep, as is that of the field of systemic therapy. It is surely a subject worthy of immersion; it has made my own work and my understanding of my responsibilities as a consultant understandable in multiple dimensions.

However, the field of public international law is not a panacea any more than systemic therapy is a panacea. Nevertheless, as practitioners interested in multilateral work across global contexts, we would do well to understand how public international law informs our international systems. We should attend deeply and robustly to understanding how it informs our very own body of practice, provoking us to find ourselves and perhaps, become that new breed of professional who is best suited to deal with world problems (Skouteris, personal communication, 2009a).

Public international law is a living, breathing thing, a dynamic process that defines and affects our lives in innumerable ways. Yet there can be no successful model of public international law without the consideration of both state and community. Most progressive values have not come up through states or treaties but through the practice of *states in the community*. This is surely something all systemic therapists can appreciate; it is the community, the systemic interactional process of relationships between people, by which we develop our values and our progress, our hopes, as a citizenry of a state, as well as the community of states.

Notes

1   Article 38:

> 1. The Court, whose function is to decide in accordance with inter-national law such disputes as are submitted to it, shall apply: a. inter-national conventions, whether general or particular, establishing rules expressly recognized by the contesting states; b. international custom, as evidence of a general practice accepted as law; c. the general principles of law recognized by civilized nations; d. subject to the provisions of Article 59, judicial decisions and the teachings of the most highly qualified publicists of the various nations, as subsidiary means for the determination of rules of law. 2. This pro-vision shall not prejudice the power of the Court to decide a case *ex aequo et bono*, if the parties agree thereto.
>
> www.icj-cij.org/en/statute

2   There are an estimated 5,000 bilateral, trilateral, multilateral and global treaties existing today. Treaties are created in small working groups, and are an expression of the will of the states who are signatories. However, of course, not all states participate equally. There are many ways of abro-gating a treaty. Further, some treaties have reservations, meaning, states can choose to agree to some articles and reserve agreement on others. Some treaties do not allow reservations, e.g. treaty on the Law of the Sea.

References

Bassiouni, M. C. (2011). *Crimes against humanity: Historical evolution and contemporary application*. New York: Oxford University Press.

Cassese, A. (1999). Moving toward international legitimation of forcible humanitarian countermeasures in the world community. *EJIL*, 10, 23.

Charlés, L., & Blair, J. (May, 2006). *Family treatment with survivors of political torture, refugees, & asylum seekers*. Florida Association for Marriage and Family Therapy Annual Conference, Palm Beach Gardens, FL.

Charlés, L. L., Moebus, P., Beechinor, L., Pearce, T., & Putney, H. (2014). Getting comfortable as "fish out of water": Using qualitative research methods training to build the technical capacity of family therapy trainees. *Journal of Marital and Family Therapy*, 40 (2), 233–245.

Charlés, L., & Singer, M. (June, 2005). *Overcoming Relational Dilemmas in Therapy and Supervision*. American Family Therapy Association

(AFTA)-International Family Therapy Association (IFTA) Conference, Washington, D.C.

Charlés, L. L. (2015). Scaling up family therapy in fragile, conflict-affected states. *Family Process, 54*, 545–558. doi:10.1111/famp.12107

Chesterman, S., Franck, T., & Malone, D. (2008). *Law and practice of the United Nations.* Oxford: Oxford University Press.

Cryer, R., Friman, H., Robinson, D., & Wilmshurst, E. (2007). *An introduction to international criminal law and procedure.* New York: Cambridge University Press.

Karns, M. P., & Mingst, K. A. (2010). *International organizations: The politics and processes of global governance.* Boulder, CO: Lynne Rienner Publishers.

Kennedy, D. W. (1985). Spring break. *Texas Law Review, 63* (8), 1377–1423.

Kennedy, D. (2004). *The dark side of virtue: Reassessing international humanitarianism.* Princeton, NJ: Princeton University Press.

Korhonen, O. (1996). New international law: Silence, defence or deliverance? *EJIL, 7* (1), 1–28.

Koskenniemi, M. (2003). What is international law for? in Malcolm Evans (Ed.), *International law.* New York: Oxford University Press.

Koskenniemi, M. (2009) The politics of international law—20 years later. *EJIL, 20* (1), 7–19.

Laszloffy, T., & Habekost, J. (2010). Using experiential tasks to enhance cultural sensitivity among MFT trainees. *Journal of Marital and Family Therapy, 36* (3), 333–346.

Schabas, W. (2012). *Unimaginable atrocities: Justice, policy, and rights at the War Crime Tribunals.* New York: Oxford University Press.

Skouteris, T. (2009b). *The notion of progress in international law discourse.* New York: Springer.

United Nations. (June 26, 1945). *Charter of the United Nations and Statute of the International Court of Justice.*

United Nations, International Law Commission. (May 23, 1969). *Vienna Convention on the Law of Treaties.*

4

INTERNATIONAL ECONOMICS AND GLOBAL EXCHANGES OF KNOWLEDGE IN FAMILY THERAPY

Writing a chapter about international economics in a book about family therapy in some ways reminds me of the wisdom of my dear friend Muriel Singer. Muriel and I went to school together to get our doctorates in family therapy; she was a true international in the way she inspired me, and inspires me still, to live and work in the world.

Muriel and I talked about many things over the years, but one of the more recent conversations I remember having with her in the years before her death in 2019 was our fascination with the country of Bhutan's measure of Gross National Happiness (GNH). The idea of GNH is in contrast to its counterpart, the more traditional Gross Domestic Product (GDP), which measures the value of goods and services produced in a country. Bhutan's GNH measures the country's development and growth in terms of health and wellness, rather than its production and income. The point of devising a measure of GNH refers to the idea that sustainable development should take a holistic approach towards notions of progress and give equal importance to non-economic aspects of well-being (OECD, 2019).

The idea of measuring a nation's well-being, its GNH rather than its GDP, may seem a bit obvious to an audience of mental health professionals. However, it may also be somewhat confounding to think through. How, exactly, does someone go about measuring happiness? How is "happiness" correlated with a country's economic growth? How do we measure growth in that way? In fact, GDP is today considered by many social scientists too blunt a measure, which does not allow us to put a value on the investment needed in health, education and social welfare in order to promote well-being.

Measuring the happiness and economic welfare of sovereign states requires a different set of tools, an interdisciplinary language and terminology, which when combined can help us investigate key international economic and policy questions in addition to questions of psychosocial health and well-being. Considering a measure of GNH requires a systemic, holistic framework—one that includes, rather than excludes, conceptual underpinnings of the GDP. Fortunately, this seems to be a growing area of social science research, as other countries adopt such well-being budgets. Muriel was right on the money about that.

Economic Growth and Challenges for States

International economists bring a powerful set of tools to their analysis of a country's growth and development, and the issues and challenges raised by the economic interactions between sovereign states. Their tools allow for the analysis and the measure of a country's terms of trade; its capital flows, liquidity, assets and debt; the price of money in a country and its reserves of foreign currency; and the freedom and attractiveness of its financial markets. Each of these factors have something to tell about how a state imagines its growth and how it conceptualizes families and their health and well-being.

Perhaps the most fundamental measure of a state's economy is its GDP. GDP can be defined as a measure of the total value of goods and services that are produced in a state's economy. A state's GDP can tell you a lot about the place, even if it doesn't tell you everything you want to know. For example, if you know a country's GDP you automatically know something about the size of its economy, and the sources of its aggregrate spending or demand. It can be useful to know what percentage of national income is spent on a country's health care, for example— especially in comparison to something else, like its military. Some countries rely a great deal on remittances, which can tell you about family ties and connections in addition to that state's economic conditions. Disasters, such as pandemics or epidemics, illustrate how graphically an economy can contract in unexpected ways. GDP is one way to measure that contraction.

When I was a Peace Corps Volunteer in Togo, I learned about the notion of "the resource curse" for the first time. The resource curse refers to how a country's natural endowment can hinder its terms of trade (Frankel, 2012). Even the economies of countries with great natural wealth can shift dramatically when conditions change, such as what happens during protracted armed conflict. Conflicts weaken institutions and constrain economies, taking a severe toll on communities and families. Libya is an example that comes to mind for me of late—partly becaused I worked there briefly after the Revolution, and over two trips, I watched part of that severe toll on communities and families unfold in real time. In addition to its catastrophic economic losses, ongoing armed conflict exacerbates other conditions in a country, adding to its political instability and issues of human security. All of these conditions compound the challenges families face on a daily basis.

What Do Countries Spend on Mental Health?

Globally, if we are looking at psychosocial support and well-being, it can be useful to compare in economics terms what countries spend on mental health. In the U.S., annual spending on mental health is less than $2 USD per person. However, it is less than $0.25 USD per person in low-income countries, where 67% of financial resources are allocated to stand-alone mental hospitals, despite their association with poor health outcomes and human rights violations (WHO, 2013). These percentages and their international comparisons lead to other critical questions worth our analysis. What is the access to health care, such as trained mental health practitioners, for example, in a country, beyond the stand-alone mental hospital? What is the labor force in that country in the field of

public mental health? What hinders a state's capacity to train and prepare that labor force to meet the needs of families? What promotes its
capacity?

Knowing if a state is a high income country (HIC) or LMIC[1] is a way to
understand the size of that state's economy, and also, a beginning place to
address some of these questions. Understanding something about how
a country's economy is a "lean economy," or a "fat economy" can tell
you other useful things, too—such as how a country uses its physical
stock, how it invests in its human capital, or how it trades with other
nations. This knowledge, in turn, can help one contextualize what families experience as part of their everyday life, how or whether they can
plan for the future, and in what ways they can or cannot. There is an
epistemological coherence that arrives when one begins to analyze state
conditions in this way—families' lives in that corner of the globe can
make a different kind of sense. There is a correlation between a country's
income percentage and its protection of the polity.

Trade and International Exchanges of Knowledge in Family Therapy

Trade with other nations and trade between nations is of particular
interest to me, as I've crossed so many borders to deliver family therapy
training projects for many kinds of regional, international, and local
organizations. Initially, when I first started doing this work, I did not
think of it as international trade. I am less sanguine about that today,
as indeed I am part of the flow of goods, ideas and people that defines
globalization. In the early days, I did not see the international system
machinations in what I was doing. I merely received an invitation or a
request, and a contract; I traveled somewhere to perform a service or a set
of tasks and scope of work; I returned home.

However, after enough of a critical mass of internatonal projects,
I began to think with more breadth and depth about the nature of these
requests, including the funding streams that supported each project.
Many projects seemed to have so much money; others had so very little.
I also began to think more critically about the international partnerships
in which the projects were embedded. For instance, as I've written elsewhere, why was I more likely to do a semester long family therapy

training course in the Philippines, and only a half-day one in Burundi? (Charlés & Bava, 2020).

Questions about exchanges of technology are also of great interest to those who specialize in international, political, and development economics. From the view of international economics professionals, it's hard to describe a world in which everyone is not interacting (Kowalcyzk, 2006). Systemic family therapists are quite likely to agree! International economics is inherently interested in the relational process of interacting economies of sovereign states. Theoretically, and in aggregate, these exchanges—"trade"—create benefits for all parties. However, on the ground, theory can become another story.

How does international trade contribute to the welfare of states? Theoretically, trade expands a country's "feasibility set"—it creates possibilities, choices, that did not exist before. "Growth," in economics terms, refers to an increase in a nation's capacity to produce a good or a service. However, trade by itself does not necessarily lead to increased growth. The capacity for growth must be *realized*. Further, the *opportunity* to trade is not the same thing as the *certainty* to trade. Finally, even if there are gains from trade, there are always differences in those gains in income (or, perhaps, in happiness) amongst particular groups *within* nations. As my colleague Gameela Samarasinghe and I wrote:

> In the parlance of international trade, and specifically knowledge transfer (which is in a sense the trade of knowledge and technical skills across borders), there is an inherent assumption that knowledge is a good that "belongs to the world." Yet like all other goods, knowledge is not equally distributed across the globe: its allocation is inefficient. Further, its distribution is highly specific to conditions on the ground. Whom is the knowledge transferred from, and whom to, exactly? What does that transfer look like in the field? What conditions inhibit or promote it?
>
> (Charlés & Samarasinghe, 2016, p. 6)

An assumption in international economics is that gains from trade best occur when partners are able to strike an exchange in which there is nothing left on the table. However, what is on the table to begin with? Why are "poor" developing countries "poor" in the first place? International economists posit that countries that are "poor," in terms of their "lean" economy, may not have a large amount of "stuff" (goods, products, or services, technology or a natural endowment) to trade. Another reason posited for lack of wealth creation in a country is that the terms of trade in that country are not attractive.

A country may have a great natural resource (and thus, a possible "resource curse") such as bauxite, but does not have the technology to devote to its extraction. Or, it does have the access to extract the bauxite, perhaps through a trade in technology, but the allocation of the gains from that trade, i.e, the distribution of the wealth from that natural resource, is allocated inefficiently. A country's terms of trade are not attractive when there is political instability, whether the cause of that is ongoing armed conflict, or a pandemic. Essentially, whether you trade a lot or a little depends on your conditions on the ground. This idea is something every systemic family therapist can inherently understand and appreciate.

"Technology transfer," a term common in international trade, is the process by which skills and technical expertise are deliverables as a "product," literally "transferred" from one set of people to another. In my work, I am usually delivering a service, or knowledge transfer, that is designed to help others deliver a service in their country. In the field of family therapy, when we cross borders to participate in the delivery of such a capacity building project, we are sharing our technical knowledge in a structured way, with the belief that "knowledge belongs to the world." We do so with the same international economist's assumptions that the sharing of such technology has the potential to increase overall well-being in a country, through the capacity building of that country's human and social capital.

Overseas Development Assistance

Post-conflict countries, which has been one of my primary areas of work as a consultant over the years, are often the recipient of international development projects. Overseas development assistance (ODA) refers to exchanges between countries, that is often undertaken by the official government sector, with the promotion of economic development and welfare as a main objective. It is typically offered in three forms: (1) Goods; (2) Factors of Production; (3) Technology. Goods are products;

Factors of production are the labor and mechanisms required to make products; Technology refers to any information that improves *the means of production.*

Technology in international trade and economics may focus on services specific to human and social capital, including the training of labor and the delivery of services. The information that I share in training with participants in Country M, for example, theoretically improves the factors of production for the health services to families that they are asked to deliver as part of their work role and organizational mission.

While much of overseas development assistance can be measured in terms of its economic growth and development, it is not always clear how mental health as an instrument of a country's development—its GNH and its GNP—is measured in terms of its efficient delivery. How does one thing lead to the other? What are the obstacles, challenges, or opportunities? In what way does it improve the conditions on the ground? Which conditions? For whom? How can we promote (if we can) the distribution of its allocation?

Promoting an Economy of Well-Being in Systemic Terms

In the field of family therapy and the related mental health professions, we are clear about our goal to make sure that any technology assistance we offer is based on adequate research, informed by the evidence base. This is certainly a step in the right direction. Ideally and theoretically, this work results in improved outcomes across every sector, and in the aggregate, can promote a state's economic equilibrium and growth.

Along these lines, it is interesting that there is a growing consensus among economists that we are looking at growth and wealth creation in a limited manner. It is limited because it is not representative of the current global economy, which is much larger than it was when the concept of GDP was introduced. A blunt view of growth such as GDP tends to be linear rather than circular, and does not account for the costs of "growth" to families and communities.

Raworth (2017) posits that the next century of economists are already figuring out how to do it differently, and "will seek to redistribute the sources of wealth by harnessing the power of the commons, including the wealth that lies in controlling land and resources, the creation of money, and in owning enterprise, technology and knowledge." The doughnut economics model Raworth (ibid.) envisions is one that allows us to consider all of the systemic complexity in which people actually live.

In this chapter, I have talked about international economics and trade in the most broad form. Having a rudimentary understanding of international trade and economics as it applies to multilateral family therapy work may also help you understand the conceptual spine of how development projects work across the globe, and how state economies interact (or if not, why not) for the benefit of family health and psychosocial support. Economies and trade always work in concert with, and in relationship to, other conditions in a country. Systemic family therapists who wish to work internationally can and should engage in this arena to better understand and contribute to this work.

It remains unclear what are the aspects of economic efficiency on the ground in family focused multilateral projects, in both the measure of "national happiness" as well as "national income." Understanding the conditions on the ground that occur during such an exchange is an area of research ideal for family therapists interested in efficient and meaningful international work.

Knowing something about the conditions inherent in a middle-income country, for example, will help you as a consultant contextualize what you are seeing when you engage with a family who lives there. Knowing something about the differences between states' economies and their international trade with other states will inform in some interesting ways how to think about one's own role in this work, as well as how to engage in multilateral projects. Knowing some key details about a state's economic conditions may mean that one is less likely to suggest a program design that fits a high-income country better than the lower-middle income country for which it is planned. This can mean asking better informed questions, so that one's contribution to an international project can be realized in a more informed way.

Note

1 The labels LMIC or HIC or FCS are not interchangeable; they are not meant to refer to people, to families, or to communities. A low-income family or community is not the same thing as a low-income country.

Always, the labels LMICs and UMICs and HICs refer to state economies. The labels are unique, they can and do change, and they define conditions worth our appreciation and understanding. One reason they are useful is their precision—they are much more specific than previous descriptors used to refer to the differences in state characteristics. There are the risks associated with particular economies. For example, middle-income countries face different risks than low income countries—precisely because of their shift toward increased production and industrialization.

References

Charlés, L., & Bava, S. (2020). Family therapy & global mental health: Reflections on professional development and training. In M. Rastogi & R. Singhe (volume Editors; K. Wampler, series editor), *Handbook of systemic family therapy, Volume IV*. New York: Wiley.

Charlés, L., & Samarasinghe, G. (2016). *Family therapy in global humanitarian contexts: Voices and issues from the field*. New York: Springer.

Frankel, J. A. (2012) Working paper: The natural resource curse: A survey of diagnoses and some prescriptions. *Commodity price volatility and inclusive growth in low-income countries*, R. Arezki, C. Pattillo, M. Quintyn & M. Zhu (Eds.). International Monetary Fund. Available at: www.nber.org/papers/w15836. National Bureau of Economic Research, Cambridge, MA: Author.

Kowalcyzk, C. (2006). Liberalizing trade between large and small: The welfare from three different strategies. *Asia-Pacific Journal of Accounting & Economics, 13*, 171–179.

Raworth, K. (2017). *Doughnut economics: Seven ways to think like a 21st-century economist*. London: Cornerstone.

Organization for Economic Cooperation and Development (OECD). (2019). *The economy of well-being—OECD background paper*. https://data.consilium.europa.eu/doc/document/ST-10414-2019-ADD-1/en/pdf

World Health Organization. (2013). *Mental health action plan 2013–2020*. Geneva, Switzerland: Author.

5

A REVIEW OF BEST PRACTICES AND INTERNATIONAL STANDARDS

Not too many years ago, I worked on a project in a city that was new to me, but in a region that was not. My work was fairly simple, at least on paper. I was hired to provide supervision support to community health workers in a country I will call Country M. Providing this kind of this supervision support was not new for me; I was also quite familiar with the population that the organization focused on in its mission and daily work. I was new to the project, but many of the practices in the medium-size organization felt familiar: Organizing supervision sessions, creating role-plays and modules to promote psychosocial skills, and developing training. The only thing that was different for me was the location, and becoming accustomed to the surrounding environment.

One day, I arrived to the office to find none of the equipment working. The utilities had not been paid; the lights were off, too. Staff had not been paid. It seemed that the NGO had run out of money before the month ended. Perhaps more money would come in a month, when new funding streams and more donations were likely to arrive? The staff continued to work, even without pay.

There were more complications. I learned that one of the health workers, a person I was supervising, had been conducting research interviews with a set of unaccompanied minors. The NGO had provided money to these minors as an incentive for their interviews. The money had come from an entity in Europe, and was part of a project that preceded my arrival at the site. I had not known of this project. The European entity did not seem to know about me, either; they had never been to Country M. Later, I learned that one of the organization's board members had arranged for the entity's research project to take place in Country M.

It was all so very confusing. I found myself wondering about everything. The strange confluence of the events nearly undid me, and I was not sure how to handle it. What I did know, or felt confident enough to speak up about, was that my supervisee was not trained to perform a professional service with this vulnerable population. Neither were they competent to work with the issues the children brought. Officially, I could affirm, the issues were beyond their training, level of experience, and competence. Yet, they were holding themselves out to do the work, not because it was on their agenda but because it was on everyone else's. What was I to do?

"The International System is Anarchy": Beyond Codes of Professional Practice

This story, though I've embellished it, is an uncomfortable one to tell. It is also much too common. Ethics and ethical issues are complex in international work, precisely because of the nature of the international system. I remember a professor saying to us once at Fletcher, "The international system is anarchy." Indeed, the scenario above reflects that anarchy. What country takes precedence in a project where there is more than one involved? How is that decided? Is it because their purse is bigger? Or because they have people on the ground? And what of the people "on the ground"? Do the host country nationals, on the ground in a way that is beyond the capacity of any foreign expat researcher or supervisor, have a say? What should come next in the scenario? Indeed, anarchy is a perfect word.

Although I am accountable to the regulatory bodies in the states where I am licensed, and the code of ethics of AAMFT, my home professional organization, the trainees I work with and colleagues I partner with in multilateral projects are unlikely to be. I use my code of practice to guide my work; however, I cannot reasonably expect others to know them and to do so, unless of course, they are also members of the same organization, or licensed by the same regulatory body. Multiple states and collaborative partners also mean multiple professional codes. This raises so many complex issues about what are standards, and what are norms? Whose standards? Whose norms?

In multilateral projects, we may be located or working with partners in a state without a set of codified national standards for mental health practice. Not every state has a clear set of guidelines to follow, such as a mental health law, or ethical/regulatory bodies, or professional associations specific to public mental health. Furthermore, regulatory bodies are certainly not the only way to establish best practice norms (Gross, 1978).

Attaching International Norms Identified as Best Practice to Our Own as Systemic Family Therapists

In these cases, local actors may rely on the parallel entities at the international level—guidelines codified by the U.N. and its organs, international law, or international norms. Indeed, it is these things that could also be identified as "best practice." I need to know about these norms. Best practices are often standard to an era, yet the complexities which challenge them are dynamic, constantly in flux, requiring one to always work in relation to the broader political and economic factors in the country (Batniji, Van Ommeren & Saraceno, 2005). Further, "[m]ental health strategies and interventions for treatment, prevention and promotion need to be based on scientific evidence and/or best practice, taking cultural considerations into account" (WHO, 2013, p. 10).

Working amongst other partners and colleagues in multilateral contexts means having a strong fluency of the larger system on the world stage of psychosocial practices, including, for example, the missions of the World Health Organization and other organs of the United Nations, and often, the World Bank Group, and the IMF, and also, regional as well as international organizations. As international norms deftly influence projects and state behavior, affecting citizens as well as project beneficiaries, knowledge of the international system and norms specific to health and mental health only enhances our capacity.

However, our systemic family therapy knowledge, skills, and attitudes are critical to bring, as well. Yet, we must adapt them to the international plane. Otherwise, we are in danger of replicating already existing inequities (Charlés, 2015). I find that the work of Carmen Knudson-Martin, Teresa McDowell & Maria Bermudez (2017 and 2019), on developing attunement to integrate clinicians' attention to the larger society processes that address social equity, is compelling and relevant to multilateral work.

I have also found it very helpful to become familiar and engaged with a number of meaningful repositories on the web, such as the Mental Health and Psychosocial Support Network, the Mental Health Innovation Network, IRIN, and ACAPS. Many norm-setting groups, such as the Inter-Agency Standing Committee (IASC) or the Sphere Project, exist for the very purpose of filling in gaps and providing information about best practices, informed by the evidence base. They are very present on the international plane. In particular, I refer a great deal to the work of the IASC Reference Group for Mental Health and Psychosocial Support in Emergency Settings (IASC, 2010).

The Inter-Agency Standing Committee (IASC) brings together international organizations working to provide humanitarian assistance to people in need as a result of natural disasters, conflict-related emergencies, global food crises and pandemics. By coordinating activities, members improve overall service delivery, share resources, pool analysis and disseminate best practices. Participants use the forum to agree on system-wide policies to achieve a better overall response, while respecting organizations' individual mandates. Established by UN General Assembly resolution 46/182 in 1991, the IASC is the only decision making group that includes UN agencies, the World Bank, the International Organization for Migration and other humanitarian organizations, such as the International Committee of the Red Cross, the International Federation of the Red Cross and Red Crescent Societies and nongovernmental organizations. In other words, the IASC includes many of the largest humanitarian organizations that account for the majority of humanitarian assistance distributed worldwide.

(OCHA, 2012)

The codes of ethics of the various mental health disciplines are not irrelevant to the multilateral work I do; however, their relevance is quite different on the international plane. They are only on one side of the Janus face, whereas our project focus is on both. Yet, I find there is a symmetry between how I use my code of ethics and also, how I use and think about the various international standards that apply to this discussion. There is a uniformity across standards and norms, which resonates for me from the systemic sensibility that is so inherent to our relational understanding of the world.

Models of MHPSS intervention differ but best practice focuses on capacity building of civil society, scaling up human resources, and sustainable practice (as defined by the UN in 1987). These are addressed specifically by methods of Scale, Skill Mix, and Task Shifting. They are unique forms of best practice, because they are essentially focused on an ethics of sustainability, as defined by the United Nations (1987).

Scale, Skill Mix, and Task-Shifting

Scale, and the concept of scaling up, refers to human resource development objectives that increase the number of people receiving services (coverage) and increase the range of services offered (e.g. family intervention methods). Addressing scalability is best done after analyzing the conditions that could hinder as well as enhance a project's success. Two ways scalability can be addressed include using a "skill mix" and "task-shifting." The concepts are useful to understand, because they can determine a project's potential to be replicated, and its likelihood of being implemented along a continuum that fits the varying and changing needs in a state. They are both a guide to best practices, in their form as well as their content.

Skill mix refers essentially to cross- trans- or inter-disciplinary training—the "technology transfer" discussed in the previous chapter. Training that focuses on the various settings in which mental health care can be delivered, and which is also cross-disciplinary is a consistent effective practice (Kakuma, Minas, Ginneken, Dal Poz, Desiraju, Morris & Scheffler, 2011). In this model, there must be meaningful focus on supervision and ongoing professional development opportunities for workers across different settings, as a way to provide and develop the important kind of "skill mix" for citizens that is needed. In certain contexts, this is almost always more effective than trying to increase the number of base professionals.

Task shifting, also known as task-sharing, is a scaling up strategy used in public mental health that engages professionals trained in other specializations (such as psychiatry, nursing, or international human rights law) to provide services to families. Task-shifting/task-sharing is a response to provide comprehensive mental health care services (such as family therapy), when state budgets do not provide necessary infrastructure for capacity building, a very common occurrence in LMICs and FCS.

Task shifting involves "delegating tasks to existing or new cadres with either less training or narrowly tailored training" (Kakuma et al., 2011, p. 16), and is a recommended action in countries with human resource challenges in mental health professions. It can be seen as an economically efficient practice, but for me, most importantly, it is considered a sustainable practice, which is: "meeting the needs of the present without compromising the ability of future generations to meet their own needs" (UN, 1987, p. 37).

Cross-Disciplinary Approaches Are Critical

Cross-disciplinary approaches that use existing infrastructures are an effective response to shortages in human resources for mental health, which are pervasive in middle and low-income countries (Patel, 2012, 2014). Kakuma et al. (2011) noted that all countries of low and middle income have inadequate funding for mental health, and that "all low-income countries and about two-thirds of middle-income countries had far fewer mental health workers to deliver a core set of mental health interventions than were needed" (ibid, p. 2). Focusing on scaling up within this set of conditions can be very effective. For me, this is one of the most critical best practice standards when it comes to working in multilateral projects.

According to the principles set out in the preamble of the Constitution of the World Health Organization: "Health is a state of complete physical, mental and social well-being and not merely the absence of disease or infirmity." Yet, how that state of well-being is manifest in its larger context is a deeply profound, not always knowable thing. It can be challenging to define, to grasp; we may struggle to know and do what is right. Ethical codes and international norms are critical to guide our multilateral work. Yet, these are contextual in how they can be applied. Sometimes, it is country specific, guided by cultural norms. Other times, it is state conditions that specify what can be done. Many times, it is the culture of the implementing organization, raising yet more questions about leadership and teams, streams of funding, and international politics. At times, I have used a combination of ethical code guidelines, best practices, and peer or legal consultation to manage especially complex dilemmas.

Global Mental Health: Bridging Gaps in Equity, Practice, and Implementation

One clear set of norms about international standards for mental health and psychosocial support is the research and body of literature on global mental health. Global mental health is the "study, research, and practice of the application of principles that place a priority on improving health and achieving equity in health for all people worldwide" (Patel & Prince, 2010). The focus of global mental health practice is often strongest in low- and middle- income countries , "which are home to over 80% of the global population, but command less than 20% of the share of the mental health resources" (ibid., p. 1976).

At its essence, global mental health is focused on bridging gaps. These gaps are pervasive, persistent and ubiquitous. Gaps in mental health access are divergent, and the way they manifest themselves will differ across states and populations. Over a decade since its inception in 2007, today in global mental health there is a substantial body of research evidence on effective psychotherapeutic interventions with specific populations or problem sets in particular countries or regions.

In my work as a family therapist, I am particularly interested in the gaps around family-focused mental health and psychosocial support in ongoing, or recent armed conflict. So, rather than tell you more about the work I am interested in, I have a question for you. Where do you want to focus your attention, as a professional interested in international work? What does your focus look like from inside where you live and work? What does it look like outside, on the flip side of the Janus face, at the international, global level? Do you see gaps? What are they? How can you learn more about them? If you are interested in working globally, what does that gap look like on the international plane? How is it being addressed already? This is a place to begin in clarifying best practice standards for the type of international work you want to do.

Mental health disorders are a key emphasis in global mental health. However, there is also substantial focus on the everyday problems of people across settings, and, in particular, how to mitigate the social determinants of mental "ill-health" (ibid). The social determinants part of the equation is important to emphasize. It is something all systemic clinicians familiar with "larger systems" (Imber-Black, 1988) will understand. Although there is conceptual agreement in global mental health that implementing programs must fit citizens' psychosocial needs without further problematizing their lives, sometimes it is not always clear how to do that. In my experience, this is particularly true with regard to family systems. Most of the extant research is focused on individuals, or members of family systems, rather than the family system itself. Fortunately, this is changing.

Do Not Forget State Conditions

One of the many challenges of working multilaterally is becoming accustomed to the conditions in states, HICs as well as LMIC or FCVs, and working within them in a focused way. State conditions may mean that there may not be rule of law, separation of powers, or constitutional freedom for citizens. What does that mean for this state's citizens? How does that inform a project? This was key to my way of dealing with the above scenario; the knowledge of state conditions helped me be quite practical about what I could or could not do. As with a family assessment, in assessing state conditions we do our best to get a clear picture of what is happening in the system at the moment of our engagement with it. However, we must look broadly, at macro as well as micro interactions. Good intentions to do well are simply not enough; they do not ensure efforts that are actually beneficial to the population. Indeed, they can be harmful.

Knowledge of best practices in family therapy, including the role of evidence-based research in the field, is a minimum necessity when working multilaterally. The extant evidence base in family therapy is replete with evidence-based strategies and interventions, which are both "change mechanisms that underlie positive clinical outcomes" and "across methods and specific to certain approaches" (Stratton, 2016, p. 417). In global mental health projects, all of our tacit knowledge must be transported and understood in a setting that, by its very nature, may be foreign to us. To build our understanding, we must develop an informed, working knowledge of global systems about states, governance, and international organizations.

As with a family in a first session, the same rules of interaction apply in international work—one always needs their flexibility, sensitivity, balance. But in this case, the context is likely to exist without the set of rules we are familiar with in our typical family therapy training milieu. It is not just one therapy room we are working in, nor one team. Rather, working multilaterally in international projects means there are many people "in the room," and also, many teams, all operating at the same moment as you.

References

Batniji, R., van Ommeren, M., & Saraceno, B. (2005). Mental and social health in disasters: Relating qualitative social science research and the Sphere standard. *Social Science and Medicine, 62,* 1853–1864.

Charlés, L. L. (2015). Scaling up family therapy in fragile, conflict-affected states. *Family Process, 54* (3), 545–558.

Gross, S. J. (1978). The myth of professional licensing. American Psychologist, 33 (11), 1009–1016.

IASC Reference Group for Mental Health and Psychosocial Support in Emergency Settings. (2010). *Mental health and psychosocial support in humanitarian emergencies: What should humanitarian health actors know?* Geneva, Switzerland: World Health Organization.

Imber-Black, E. (1988). *Families and larger systems: A family therapist's guide through the labyrinth.* New York: Guilford Press.

Kakuma, R., Minas, H., Ginneken, N., Dal Poz, M. R., Desiraju, K., Morris, J., & Scheffler, R. M. (2011). Human resources for mental health care: Current situation and strategies for action. *Lancet*, *378,* 1654–1663.

Knudson-Martin, C., McDowell, T., & Bermudez, J. M. (2019). From knowing to doing: Guidelines for socioculturally attuned family therapy. *Journal of Marital and Family Therapy*, *45,* 47–60. https://doi.org/10.1111/jmft.12299

McDowell, T., Knudson-Martin, C., & Bermudez, M. (2017). Ethics of socioculturally attuned family therapy: Beyond diplomacy. AAMFT Annual Conference, Atlanta, GA.

Office for the Coordination of Humanitarian Affairs, (31 Mar 2012) OCHA on Message: Inter-Agency Standing Committee [EN/AR]. Accessed at: https://reliefweb.int/report/world/ocha-message-inter-agency-standing-committee-enar

Patel, V. (2012). Global mental health: From science to action. *Harvard Review of Psychiatry*, *20* (1), 6–12.

Patel, V. (2014). Why mental health matters to global health. *Transcultural Psychiatry*, *51,* 777–789.

Patel, V., & Prince, M. (2010). Global mental health: A new global health field comes of age. *JAMA*, *303* (19), 1976–1977.

Stratton, P. (2016). *The evidence base of family therapy and systemic practice.* Warrington, UK: Association for Family Therapy.

United Nations. (1987). *Gather a body of global agreements. Our common future, Chapter. 2, Towards Sustainable Development, a/42/47, Annex.* UN Documents.

World Health Organization (2013). *Mental health action plan 2013–2020.* Geneva: World Health Organization.

6

REFLECTING ON INTERVENTION

Moral Hazards of Multilateral Work

In April of 2018, I went to the Spring Meetings held every year at the World Bank in Washington, D.C. Part of this international conference, free and open to the public, was a series of sessions on Fragility, Conflict, and Violence. On the last afternoon, I went to hear a panel featuring the economist and Oxford scholar Paul Collier (2018).[1] The panel was the reason I had attended the conference, as Collier's book *The Bottom Billion* (Collier, 2007) has been influential for me for a number of years. I knew how compelling he was as a writer. However, I was struck to find him even more mesmerizing as a speaker. The clarity with which he spoke was so resonant for me, especially when he talked about the role of foreigners in fragile states. I wrote his comments down furiously in my small notebook.

"Foreigners cannot save a society," Collier said, with an air of authority and resignation at the same time. "Outsiders can help, but it's the society that has to do it. A large majority of the citizens in the society." In the cavernous conference room at the World Bank, Collier's vehemence and declarations were seared in my memory, and in the all caps letters in my notebook. "We know so little [about fragile, conflict affected states] and they are all so different. We don't know better than they do." As if he knows we need to hear him repeat the point, he adds, "They are in a better position than we are to know."

At one point, a brave and eager participant raised his hand to ask a question: "Maybe it's inequality in those places that has created the fragility?" (I think the country we were speaking of at that moment was Yemen.) Collier was having none of it. "That is just a Western retrofit—a form of moral imperialism. It's a curse! And we should stop doing it." I was writing furiously in my notebook. Collier then went on to speak about why we need to "treat the features of fragility that are interdependent and mutually reinforcing, why we need to 'think forward rather than backward.'"

The forcefulness with which Collier spoke that day was in such contrast to his understated presence and the formality of the meetings. His posh English accent, his seersucker suit and white hair, his unprepossessing gait and scholarly glasses—all of it took a backseat to the words he spoke. Now, if I had not read Paul Collier's book, nor felt familiar with the body of his work in the context of international economics, I think I would have been slightly put off by his comments that day. I would not have been able to be curious. However, I was not put off, and I was indeed very curious. In fact, I was delighted. His words energized me.

As a family therapist based in the U.S., I appreciate so much the critical voice on intervention that Paul Collier brought to the discussions at the World Bank that day. He is of course, in his work, intervening. He is himself in an expert role at the World Bank. In his work in fragile states, you can bet he is intervening. But, you see how he questions the intervention at the same time he discusses it, and he does it so viscerally, with such passion. I so welcomed the direct forthrightness and blazing clarity he brought to the table. It was such an apt response, quite in proportion, I felt, to the numerous unpleasant moments I have seen happen in multilateral projects, whereby a stark and often blind imposition of values can happen so easily. It's a constant risk, the imposition of values that sneaks into our effort at intervention. Collier slammed it down with such emotional force—not a very common impulse I've seen in the world of international economics. It is one I find so relatable to as a family therapist.

When I talk to family therapy graduate students who seek me out because of my international work, they often ask, "How can I do what *you* are doing?" The question is extraordinarily common, and posed with such pure, honest innocence, that I am taken aback. However, the question nevertheless leaves me feeling unsettled, in one way or another.

> Whatever your own individual motives for working in humanitarian aid, human rights, or development projects, virtually all humanitarian workers want to "make a difference" and want to "help other people." But in the real world of humanitarian work, it is not always entirely clear what helps people and what actions, though intended to help people, may actually harm them. ... These issues and work has a moral complexity...created and intensified by human actions.
>
> (Ehrenreich, 2005, p. 13–15)

Intervention brings with it an especially challenging set of moral hazards. We therapists are predisposed, perhaps, by our collective set of values, our training, our personal experiences, to intervene. Of course, our efforts to help—to work with a client, in other words—require us to intervene in one way or another. Therapy *is* itself an intervention. Clients agree to the intervention, of course, when they sign on the dotted line. Then off we go, into the territory of intervention. There, right away, the moral hazards begin.

States, too, agree to intervention in multilateral projects. However, in multilateral work, I think moral hazards are multiplied in ways that may seem unimaginable and difficult to fathom, even to the seasoned therapist. The hazards are very difficult to capture, somehow unyielding to serious examination. Collier's vehemence, for me, recognized that in a public, grave way that I want to remember.

Beware the Tyranny of Expertise

Now that I've made you perhaps curious about Paul Collier, I want to share some of the other things he said that day. Because naming a moral hazard is only the beginning; there is so much more to say, so much more to discuss. There is a reason he spoke the way he did: He has the gravitas and the receipts to make such statements. The statements need to be heard and he is a perfect one to voice them. He also has the expertise—the chops, if you will—that compel you to listen, even if you disagree.

However, if you disagree, you may have to reconcile your disagreement, because Collier also says this: "Fragile states have some of the strongest people you can imagine" (2018). Yes, of course, you might say. I'd then ask you, tell me what you know about the strongest people who are living in fragile states? Tell me what you know, what you want to understand? Only then would I ask you, what is the moral hazard of intervention, there, for you?

"There is so much talent on the ground; we must tap into the resources on the ground" —Collier (2018) reminded us in the audience that day. Sound familiar? Collier has a strengths-based focus many systemic family therapy clinicians would clearly recognize. He then asked more challenging questions, the ones you have to ask when you begin to work across states and with multiple country partners in a project. "Who will shape the future of fragile states? How can we make sure they are not fragile in the first place? How do we move from more fragile to less fragile?"

Now, insert the word "family" where "fragile states" is, and you can see how these questions are analogous to family therapy questions and intervention. Yes, we have a method of intervention, an established practice of intervention, a body of work creating a discipline that is intervention. We have established this in the U.S., where I sit here as I am writing this book. But if you wanted to work on the other side of the equation, when intervention is prevention, what would you do then? In Country X or Country M? What would you do at the international level? Amongst other partners, across a multilateral project, with multiple countries involved?

We often talk about ways to strengthen families, and relationships, in the realm of prevention. But, I'd like to know, how do you think about intervention with regard to states, across a set of events happening on the international plane? How is an effort at training public health workers in Tashkent, themselves from places like Kazakhstan, Turkmenistan, Armenia, Russia, Uzbekistan, and the Kyrgyz Republic, relevant to their institutional, as well as professional, capacity? As professionals who are also part of a special community of citizens of the former USSR, how might issues of identity and intervention be addressed in a family therapy training?

If you believed, as Collier does, that "Fragile states have some of the strongest people you can imagine," what would you want to know about those trainees' lives? How would that knowledge change the questions you ask and the approach you take?

Recognizing the Dark Side of Virtue: Reading David Kennedy, Martti Koskenniemi, and Immi Tallgren in Cairo

When I think about intervention, in the type of multilateral work I do today, I am very grateful for being introduced to the work of three people by the work of three other people, scholars whom I met when I lived in Cairo. In the fall of 2009, I took my first two classes in international human rights law (IHRL). I was a teaching faculty in Cairo at the time, and during the day I was in family therapy academia-land. At night, however, I was completely caught up in the courses on international human rights law, which took place on the campus in Tahrir Square, soon to become ground zero for the Egyptian Revolution in January 2011.

When I began to study international human rights law in Cairo, I considered myself a seasoned family therapy academic. I was published in the important journals, with an established body of work as a participatory, qualitative researcher. But I was also genuinely at a loss to explain so many things I had experienced internationally while working across the globe. I understood enough of the therapeutic, systemic content about the differences in family dynamics, and patterns, and belief systems I saw in various countries. Yet, I understood so little about the larger system of states that shaped families and communities. Cairo was the point at which I began to take a laser-sharp focus to my years of lingering, persistent questions. It was my first effort to understand the international plane with rigor, in a classroom under the tutelage of other experts.

The classes in Cairo changed my life. I had already been accepted to the Master's degree program at the Fletcher School of Law and Diplomacy (which my Cairo professors had heartily endorsed), but I had deferred that acceptance due to my departure to Cairo. I earned the Fletcher degree a few years later, but it was the set of international human rights law courses I took in Cairo the year before the revolution that really shaped my world. Every project and job I've had since that time bears the imprint of my understanding it through the nature of international law, and the scholars of it that I met in Cairo.

The Cairo international human rights law faculty, esteemed scholars in their own right, with doctorates in law from places like Harvard and Leiden University, were, like me, mid-career professionals. We were peers in that we both worked for the same institution, but I found we were alike in other ways, too. To my delight, I found a strong symmetry in their postmodern critiques, appraisals, and discourse about international law.

The IHRL courses also felt so familiar to me—the reflexivity, the critical thinking, and the irreverence, too. My professors had really sharp teaching styles, were very engaging, informed, and inquisitive. But it was the content that they brought to their courses that I want to share now. There are three readings, in particular, that have stayed with me; I will discuss two of them here. The pieces are focused on international human rights law as a field, a discipline. However, I have found each of them quite useful and applicable to my multilateral projects as a family therapist working across the globe. The first piece is by David Kennedy (1985) and the second, by Immi Tallgren (1999). I'll leave the work of the third scholar, Martti Koskenniemi, for you to seek out on your own.

David Kennedy narrates in his unforgettable piece Spring Break that one must know the "right tactic" that produces "results" in human rights work. He observes that whatever we try to produce tends to be described in a noble form. His piece too, is noble, although you can see bits of the crisis of representation (the dark side of virtue) eking out of it. There is a difference between the "remove of analysis" and the "muddle of practice," as Kennedy says, and his piece reflects that muddle, in form and content.

As Kennedy begins to describe his adventure—he was going to Latin America from Boston to do a legal evaluation of a woman activist in prison—from flight in to flight out, he shows us how humanitarian intervention on the ground is also preordained by traditional academic discourse in the field of IHRL. Everyone has a role to play and a script to follow—victims, saviors, and perpetrators. Kennedy draws us into his storytelling by first describing the stark difference between what we do in IHRL on the ground and what IHRL analysis says we should do.

Meetings with prison officials and prisoners are also plot points of rupture—when the script does not fit the planned experience. Kennedy reminds us throughout the paper, with examples, that it's the distance from the atrocity that keeps us safe in our academic narrative; the moment we are engaged on the ground, the narrative changes. I felt this piece so vividly; I'd encountered all of this in my own work as a consultant, and here Kennedy had written his piece as if not a lawyer at all, but as a therapist would write it, that is, as a human being, which I found so captivating.

I agree with Kennedy that IHRL (among other fields) finds its virtue through "safely distanced" contact with the "certifiably barbaric." As the IHRL audience, we too are complicit in this process; we are servants of the discourse, as Kennedy states. This makes me think that IHRL, from a distance, is a kind of fairy tale, in that it is always about the noble story, the happy ending, the pot of gold (human rights) at the end of the rainbow. In our quest, we encounter much travail; we slay demons; we are tested. Yet we persist. When we succeed, we write it down—hoping to inspire others. Kennedy's piece illustrates that we don't always come out of such experiences unscathed, and that even the ruptures are worth telling.

This is a piece that to me is such a cautionary tale for family therapy. We are at the beginning of this journey, looking for the noble story of our place, in international work and in global mental health settings. We see it very romantically, with brilliant good intentions. There is little evidence of any struggle we encounter as we are doing it, as Kennedy wrote, or any fist pounding on the table, demanding us to check our good intentions, as Paul Collier warned. We haven't encountered the struggle, perhaps. Not yet.

The question Immi Tallgren (1999) deals with in her piece is: How does one perform when she encounters the struggle? And what if, in the performing, she is aware of the intervention's potential harm? Tallgren asks the questions at the same time she must marginalize them, because she is participating as a working delegate in Rome, in the creation of the Rome Statute, the treaty that established the International Criminal Court. Her piece forces us to ask: How do we engage in the everyday practice of what are ultimately abstract ideals? How does one "achieve" human rights and "practice" justice? Is it possible to create a just product with not-so-just methods?

Tallgren illustrates in both the form and content of her piece the complexity and dilemmas inherent to the practice of international criminal law and international human rights law. Prosecuting perpetrators of heinous crimes causing great suffering of humanity is a high ideal with which few disagree, including Tallgren. The form of the piece takes multiple lenses, all Tallgren's various identities at the conference, and similarly, parallel viewpoints in IHRL discourse. She uses these lenses critically, to speak to her own views, and also to address multiple conundrums inherent to the practice of IHRL.

At the Rome meeting, Tallgren describes with precision the legal discourse taking place and how it reflects the tropes of years past (especially the years of Nuremberg), which hang on the contemporary stage as a kind of baggage. The meta-narrative is this: The work that takes place at the Rome conference is about the overall development of humanity. So, it is a good thing. Right? This is the trope of IHRL, after all. It is for the greater good. However, what Tallgren finds at the Rome conference is that the urge to act becomes more important than anything else (more important even than the greater good).

The unequal distribution of power between states with varying resources becomes painfully clear, as does the confusion about gender being seen as a minority group to be "protected," but both discourses are marginalized in favor of the urge to act. As Tallgren put it, "We feel strongly that the crimes we punish are unjust; therefore, we must act." Action comes from a moral urge that must be satisfied. Bartering away human rights to make concessions for other, "lesser" rights is politics— the "everyday" mechanism of international justice. It's not pretty, but it gets the job done.

It takes individual people to execute the state machinations. Putting the ideals that inform human rights and international justice into practice is work of an altogether different order—a different category of thing to be examined, deconstructed, critiqued, and questioned. This is what Tallgren achieves in her piece. In the Rome conference, she knows it is wiser to talk about how well the statute can work, rather than question that the reality on the ground may not fit the facts. But, through her paper, which reads like a deeply painful and graphic account of a surgical operation, Tallgren questions anyway. The integrity of her questions is inspiring, and frightening.

I think that in family therapy we have begun to have the inspiring part of the discourse Tallgren reflected on. We have not yet robustly examined what it means when we intervene, nor debated the moral hazards that are inherent in the role of intervention. We haven't analyzed nor fully discussed the ways that our interventions can be risky, even frightening, when they are applied, internationally, and conceptualized, globally. Our questions mostly center on the fairy tale, rather than the difficulties of the process.

"Fragile States Have Some of the Strongest People You Can Imagine"

Working across states as a family therapist raises many questions for me; my questions have changed over the years, but I don't ever expect them to disappear. When I consider answering "Yes" to a project these days, I really want to hear how the international partners talk about families, and family systems. I'm curious where *they* stand on the continuum of intervention. Are they more like 1988 Anderson and Goolishian or early Salvador Minuchin? Are they reminiscent at all of the work and sensibility of Gregory Bateson (1972)? Do they ring to me of Jay Haley? or Carl Whitaker?

I'm always pleased to see when they appreciate the complexity of systems work. However, I am also wondering (and looking to see): Can they describe or imagine the systems ideas they purport to deliver? What kind of *systems imagination* do they have? What kind of *systems listening* are they doing? In addition, I need to see that organizations have a presence on the ground in a country. If they do, what is the presence's "effect" on the ground? Do families know and trust it? Who are the actors who know about it, and how are they engaged with each other?

Sometimes, I have seen things go terribly wrong in a project. Its moral infrastructure looks good in theory and on paper, but on the ground it is glaringly absent or, worse, corrupt. I have seen things I wish I had never seen. So, you see, perhaps, why I applaud Collier. He is so correct. Moral hazards are more than a theoretical dilemma. As Tallgren reminds, the urge to act can be more urgent than the discussion of the best way to do so. I know what that looks like. In that urgency, sometimes wrongs can be righted, but not always. What, then?

After several vivid and unpleasant experiences in separate multilateral projects, I began to discern differently which projects made the most sense for me to engage in, and which did not. For me, the "best" projects—that is, the most sustainable, according to the UN definition (1988) of allowing people to meet their future needs without you—have been where there is a robust inner circle of people supporting and being supported by the work we are doing. The support can be monetary, but that is not enough. As Kaberuka (2018) put it that day at the World Bank: "Just because your project has a lot of money doesn't mean it's good; it just means it has a lot of money!"

I have worked in projects with gross amounts of money, and also projects without any money at all. For me, what stands out over and over is that there has to be moral support and commitment for a project to work, and at multiple levels. There has to be accountability on the ground, in the field, *and* upstream, at the headquarters office in whatever city it might be in—Geneva, Vienna, Berlin, Brussels, or Washington, D.C.

For me, it's fine if that accountability is in writing—usually it is, and that's great—but I also need to be convinced of it in other ways, too. I hope to see it in the people engaged—those who recruited me and those who I meet in the field. I need to hear and find the Paul Colliers and Immi Tallgrens and David Kennedys.

Also, as in systemic therapy, I work in such a way that requires I eventually become unnecessary. So, I maintain an exit-strategy mindset in multilateral projects. These projects always have discrete beginnings and endings, even if they go on for years. I will not be involved forever, nor should I be, and a project design needs to reflect that in some way. So: What is the measurable outcome we are all moving toward, and how is it tied to my understanding of the exit strategy?

Working as a family therapist means a life of questions and comfort with questions, right? I listen closely to the sincere questions of trainees and emergent family therapists who want so much to do what I do. I am faced with such unusual dilemmas that I find I ponder questions and moral hazards a great deal. There are specific types of challenges faced when one is working multilaterally. They can also, as I've learned, be analyzed and addressed multilaterally.

Note

1   Professor Paul Collier's name and my vignette about his talk at the 2018 World Bank meeting are used with his permission.

References

Anderson, H., & Goolishian, H. (1988). Human systems as linguistic systems: Preliminary and evolving ideas about the implications for clinical theory. *Family Process, 27*, 371–393.

Bateson, G. (1972). *Steps to an ecology of mind.* New York: Basic Books.

Collier, P. (2007). *The bottom billion: Why the poorest countries are failing and what can be done about it.* New York: Oxford University Press.

Collier, P. (April 16, 2018). Roundtable on state fragility and development. Spring Meetings of the International Monetary Fund (IMF) and the World Bank Group. Washington, D.C.

Ehrenreich, J. A. (2005). *The Humanitarian companion: A guide for international aid, development and human rights workers.* Rugby, Warwickshire, England: Practical Action Publishers.

Haley, J. (1973). *Uncommon therapy: The psychiatric techniques of Milton H. Erickson, M.D.* New York: W. W. Norton.

Kennedy, D. W. (1985). Spring break. *Texas Law Review, 63* (8), 1377–1423.

Kaberuka, D. (April 16 2018). Roundtable on state fragility and development. *Spring meetings of the International Monetary Fund (IMF) and the World Bank Group.* Washington, D.C.

Minuchin, S. (1974). *Families & family therapy.* Cambridge, MA.: Harvard University Press.

Tallgren, I. (1999). We did it? The vertigo of law and everyday life at the diplomatic conference on the establishment of an international criminal court. *LJIL, 12* (3), 683–707.

United Nations. (1988). *Gather a body of global agreements. Our common future, Chapter. 2, Towards Sustainable Development, a/42/47, Annex.* UN Documents.

Whitaker, C., & Bumberry, W. M. (1988). *Dancing with the family: A symbolic-experiential approach.* New York: Brunner/Mazel.

PART II

ON THE GROUND AND IN THE FIELD

7

"WE DON'T THINK OF OUR CHILDREN AS SOLDIERS"

Rehabilitation and Reintegration of Former
Child Soldiers in a Region of East Africa

In 2012, I published a paper in Family Process that illustrated my qualitative analysis of termination sessions of a therapy case with a survivor of torture, displaced to the United States after facing targeted persecution by state actors in his home country (Charlés, 2012). In that paper, I had focused on the therapy conversation exemplars about the client's perceptions of the work we had done together. In particular, the following words he spoke to me still resonate, years later:

> Well, I tried not to talk too much about the war these days because talking about the war brings some reflection and I remember all that had passed and how some people feel about it, some people in this country didn't know exactly what happened and some didn't even believe it really happened.
>
> (as cited in Charlés, 2012)

My client had been displaced to the U.S. when I wrote about him. He'd applied for asylum[1]; and he now had a safe place to call home; he was fluent in English; he was married. His previous persecution and torture had not left him with a physical disability. Nevertheless, the reason he had become a client was because of the war in his country. There would be no therapy and no client had there been no war. Nor would he have chosen to leave his home had his life not been threatened. His forced displacement had contributed to the psychosocial issues he was facing.

War and Conflict Set Off a Cascade of Events for Their Citizens

In addition to casualties, violence, and threats to health and livelihood, wars and violence destroy infrastructure and the institutions that sustain a society, such as rule of law, health care and the educational system (Phama, Vincka, and Weinstein, 2010). Violence also leads to "long-term physical, social, and psychological effects among survivors who may have lost family members, those who no longer have the means to sustain their livelihoods, or who have experienced amputation, disfigurement, displacement, torture, abduction, sexual violence, malnutrition, and disease" (ibid., p. 98).

Further, countries with histories of recent or ongoing conflict may be in the midst of a process of transitional justice, a method that "lies at the nexus of public health, conflict and social reconstruction" (Phama et al., 2010). Transitional justice refers to the range of approaches that societies moving from repressive rule or armed conflict use to reckon with legacies of widespread or systematic human rights abuse as they progress toward peace, democracy, the rule of law, and respect for individual and collective rights so as to prevent future human rights abuses (ibid.).

It is unlikely a country is negotiating only with itself and its citizens when it comes to transitional justice processes; the international community, as part of the larger system, is present or absent in ways that are useful to analyze. For many countries, depending on their geopolitical location, bilateral and regional partnerships are more relevant, whether cooperative or not, as well as those at the international level, perhaps with organs of the UN. Interdisciplinary approaches are needed to develop meaningful information about how to best meet the diverse psychosocial needs of this population (Saul & Bava, 2008; Weine, Ware & Klebic, 2004).

Psychosocial Well-Being and Former Child Combatants: Using Qualitative Research to Assess Needs

Qualitative research concepts often find their way into my multilateral work. Often, they are used informally, borrowed as a method for how I organize my notes and overall process. However, on some projects, I have been hired to use them as a methodology for a mission and deployment. In this chapter, I will focus on a project I once worked on in a community and region of East Africa, where a U.S.-based NGO—funded by another two organizations partnered in two different countries in western Europe—were collaborating to implement a program for former child combatants.

The project, funded for several years, was focused on trying to reintegrate former child soldiers back into their communities and homes. Finding deep stigma against them amongst the population, the organization decided to instead establish a safe and appropriate residential environment for the former combatants, who were still minors at the time of the project implementation. The project was informed by international norms and best practices for this population, discussed below. It was also further purposed to deliver a comprehensive range of psychosocial services and livelihood training to the beneficiaries, helping them to manage the sequelae of their experiences as child soldiers, and to reintegrate into their communities.

Consulting is often full of a "wish list" of items by the organizing partner, and this project was no different. My terms of reference involved conducting a rapid needs assessment of the local partners on the ground in the country, assessing their services, methodology, and geographical coverage. Rather more specifically, I was tasked to identify psychosocial support needs for the former combatants, and develop a work plan for their reintegration over the next several years.

The threats to psychosocial health of former child soldiers who are being reintegrated into their communities after war was not something I ever thought I would be analyzing when I trained as a family therapist.

However, today, understanding more about how to re-integrate former combatants into their family and community is a key part of several projects I'm involved in. It is an area of research scholarship studied in multiple fields, including sociology, economics and development, international human rights law, and family therapy (Amarasingam & Dawson, 2018; Monforte, 2007; Weine, 2020).

There are so many avenues whereby family systems approaches can be useful in work with former child combatants. For instance, in their open-ended interviews with 43 parents, siblings, and friends of 30 men and women who travelled to Syria and Iraq to fight with jihadist groups, Amarasingam and Dawson (2018) concluded that more needed to be done to educate families about radicalisation leading to violence. They offered the following points of interest that I think are especially relevant for systemic family therapy scholars:

> It is recognised that families are likely to be the first to detect something is happening to their child, yet the parents we interviewed, while being responsible and caring, had little sense of what they could do in the situation.
>
> (ibid., p. 22)

They further suggested there needed to be more "extensive social support to families of foreign fighters," noting in their findings that

> All the parents we interviewed had interacted with law enforcement agents, but usually found this interaction problematic. Law enforcement agents should seek to be more supportive when speaking to parents of foreign fighters, and develop better partnerships with staff in community organisations, religious leaders and social workers who could help the families cope with the child's departure. The parents need help dealing with many questions they have about why their children have left. In the absence of such help ... the parents may take matters into their own hands, placing themselves in danger and at risk of being exploited by others. Many parents end up struggling with problems with drugs, alcohol, depression and excessive grief in response to the departure, and possible death, of their children.
>
> (Amarasingam & Dawson, 2018, p. 22)

Finally, Amarasingam and Dawson note a sentiment that I think all systemic family practitioners can relate to:

> Spending time with friends and family members of foreign fighters over the last several years has been deeply educational and a heartbreaking experience in field research. As scholars of radicalisation and terrorism, we often turn these individual stories into statistics and graphs and carry out analysis. However, it is important for researchers to sit with these stories and listen to parents and friends as they narrate the lives of young people too easily demonised and caricatured. Understanding the process of radicalisation is important but understanding the larger impact a young person's choice has had on those around them is equally relevant to ongoing policy discussions and evolving research questions.
>
> (Amarasingam & Dawson, 2018, p. 23)

Assessing What Is Needed from Many Different Angles

Fragile states are characterized by dysfunctional institutions and a history of conflict, and many of their resources may be destroyed in war (Andrimihaja, Cinyabuguma & Devarajan, 2011). After war and conflict, the mental health and psychosocial support programming can be organized by nationals of a country; however, it is also likely to supported, in terms of fieldwork sites, additional training, research initiatives, and program development, by international organizations in the region. In these settings, I am often working as a liaison between organizations and people—again for me reminiscent of the larger systems and multi-sector nature of work in fragile, conflict affected countries. That is because as a consultant, I am often in a unique position to learn from many different angles.

Specifically, I often find myself gathering information that elicits clearer understanding of what sociologist Charles Tilly (2002) called a country's public politics, categorical inequality, and networks of trust. This is extremely useful in multilateral work, as it enriches contextual understanding to know something about who is included and who is excluded in the state polity, and to spend time in examination of how power is distributed. What are the relationships like between those included and excluded from state behavior? What are the boundaries between groups of citizens, and how are these boundaries negotiated, especially with regard to available resources? How do citizens manage (reduce) threat and uncertainty? Can they, and how do they, make these efforts? Are their efforts "contingent on the performance of others they cannot control" (ibid.)?

Although the community center that was planned for the former combatants had yet to be opened, I was asked to develop a training plan, interview potential staff members, and begin training newly hired mental health counselors who would provide individual and group counseling services to the beneficiaries in the center. Systemic family based therapy services was relevant to everything we were doing. In fact, it was key to the integration of the former combatants, who were stigmatized by their families for taking up with rebels during the recent conflict.

Action and Appreciation in the Field: A Stance and a Method

Part of consulting work in projects like this, for me, is also very much like action research and appreciative inquiry. We are learning as we are doing, keeping a focus on the "grand-tour" question (Spradley, 1979), while adjusting our sub-questions to fit better the circumstances we find on the ground. It helps to pay close attention to assets and resources that already exist. I remember I spent a lot of time talking to people on the ground. When I learned about previous key collaborators in similar, recent projects, I suggested we travel to interview them, across their several villages. They were difficult to reach but the NGO had a vehicle and it was doable.

In another example, I developed an interview protocol with clinical staff candidates; this serendipitously helped to further refine my understanding of what the threats were to the psychosocial support of the young former combatants they were hoping to serve. With my NGO colleagues, I drafted several SOW (scopes of work) for the residential counselors to be hired at the site, began reviewing resumes, and also, conducting the interviewing of candidates for the role of MHPSS program staff.

One of the more well-known NGOs in Europe had had a presence on the ground in this country's capital. However, they had recently ended their project and left the country, leaving behind many furloughed workers who had been trained in MHPSS. Thus, with the staff of the NGO that had brought me, I interviewed nine candidates. Many of them brought their previous training certificates, and I was surprised to see the name of a colleague, someone I knew personally, as their trainer.

My interview questions focused on asking candidates to elaborate on their ideas of working with the population, to describe the type of training they would like or think they would need. We asked them to give us an introduction to their formal education, their experiences as clinicians and/or supervisors, and for descriptions of previous experience at community sensibilisation—essentially, raising awareness and providing psychoeducation in the community. Stigma is a real issue for mental health of young people across the globe. When those young people have been combatants in a conflict, stigma seems a very insufficient description of their challenges to re-integrate into society.

Indeed, some of the current extant literature on countering violent extremism was also consistent with the candidates' views about the phenomenon of former soldiers in the country and how to help them. Following are some of the comments from my interviews with the women:

"Maybe we don't hear about it because they hide themselves...and we don't think of our children as soldiers."

"The top three needs for former child soldiers are: physical/mental health support, housing, and job training."

"The best way to help them is to show them that they have survived and overcome but also, we need to show them that they need to continue to develop."

"We have to help them have new ideas."

"We need to re-educate and re-integrate the [child] into the family, reconciliation with the family is important to bring back the child."

Several of the candidates had university degrees; many had had numerous specialized trainings (in areas such as sexual violence, violence against women, group therapy, and community mobilisation). More than one had had training experiences in a nearby, anglophone country (in English) with a Senior Advisor to the NGO. All of the candidates could articulate easily the role and basic skills of psychosocial counselors in post-conflict settings. Additionally, although each had worked for the same NGO, they had each done so in different projects, in both rural (in the "interior") areas as well as urban city. Previously, their work had spanned areas including: Working with street children, conducting research on a UNICEF child soldier project, conducting group therapy and psychoeducation in groups, working with refugees from nearby countries in the region, working with individuals who have lost part-ners to HIV, with genocide survivors, sexual and gender-based violence (SGBV) and unaccompanied minors. They were incredibly seasoned.

The furloughed counselors had mentioned specific trainings they hoped to have to meet the needs of the beneficiaries and their reintegration into the community. As it was part of my Terms of Reference (TOR) to develop a multi-year training plan, I welcomed these suggestions. The project had begun working on the development of cultural translations for mental health assessment tools (including the Harvard Trauma Questionnaire [Mollica, Caspi-Yavin, Bollini, Truong, Tor & Lavelle, 1992]) to be used in the project, and this was the heart of the training I delivered. However, in future, the workers also suggested training in crisis intervention and crisis management; trauma-informed training; and family counselling techniques. The latter was suggested for the hopeful eventuality of when the beneficiaries would be reunited with their families.

Theoretical knowledge and scholarship about child soldiers is plen-tiful; however, how could I capture this data and transform it into a set of training modules? I focused on a highlighting a systemic combin-ation of knowledge, skills, and attitudes, to do with international norms regarding former combatants, sexual and gender based violence, effects of long term exposure to war and combat, particularly for children. With the help of a colleague in the U.S., I constructed a brief module on the Paris Principles and Guidelines on children Associated with Armed Forces or Armed Groups, which builds on the 1997 Capetown Principles and Best Practices on the recruitment of children into the armed forces, and on demobilization and social reintegration of child soldiers in Africa.

Toward the end of my stay, I conducted a focus group discussion (FGD) with the trainees about their ideas for the project structure and organization. Participants offered so many interesting observations about the following special problems of children, particularly for girls, who are recruited into armed groups during war and conflict. Today I still find their observations so prescient and sound.

"Girls marry too early for security during war"

"Poverty that comes during war is because people cannot work or make money"

"Girls face increased sexual violence, unwanted pregnancy, and HIV/AIDS, and they are kicked out of the community."

The focus group ended with one member of the group summarizing:

"To overcome the problems of girl soldiers, it is the communities' responsibility. If the community doesn't change, how can the girls' situations change?"

Knowing from the Inside

In another year, in a different region of the world and on a separate project, I interviewed a young professional in Asia. He was sought out by families for social, and sometimes psychosocial, assistance after the war in their country. I was fascinated that his work had little or no involvement at all with any psychologists or counselors—whether expat or host country national. Essentially, he did simple things that took on a very complex meaning; visiting families of the disappeared, facilitating networks, and, very practically, doing interpretation and translation to connect these families with others who can help them. His work, rather than illustrating a lack of human resources in mental health, instead reflected the diverse approaches being used by a variety of professionals to "acknowledge the impact of war, repression, and human right abuses on individuals and communities" (Phama et al., 2010, p. 99).

As a professional, he could work with others inside international organizations, and in that way, put pressure on the government to meet the needs of the families who came to him (the bargaining that Tilly discusses). In a more micro-aspect, he did other things: He assisted families to file complaints; to locate their loved ones after the war; and he helped them to document news stories. Many of the people who come to him were women who had lost their husbands, a group that faces especially unique challenges to their security after a war. I asked him a question in one of our talks: What are the skills he found most necessary to be successful in his efforts. He told me clearly and without hesitation: "(1) One must know from the inside the experience of an affected group, and (2) You must be involved in changing things, and doing an action" (Charlés, 2015).

When I think about the kind of multilateral work I do today, the best practices and evidence base, the international norms and standards, and all of the acronyms and organizations that are involved, I also try to stay connected to the elegant simplicity of what this activist told me. Even in entering a new space, geopolitically new to us, or a new set of issues in a community where we are delivering an intervention, how can we "know from the inside" the experience of this affected group? For me, qualitative research, particularly ethnographic approaches and methods, are critical. The involvement in changing things, doing an action, matters, too— but I find for helping professionals like myself it must also be tempered with an extreme sensitivity. Of course, a systemic approach is needed to design and deliver mental health and psychosocial support projects in international settings. Such an approach should include "interdisciplinary and multi-sectoral collaborations and strong partnerships between government ministries, researchers, nongovernmental organisations, health professionals, affected individuals or caregivers, and communities ..." (Tol, Patel, Tomlinson, Baingana, Galappatti, and Panter-Brick, 2011, p. 98).

System concepts, participatory methods of assessment, and an ecological approach, incorporating family and community (Song, Tol & de Jong, 2014; Weine, 2011) are instrumental to multilateral work. However, there is always more to know, and also, many ways to know. Face to face contact in the field can provide key opportunities to better understand the public politics, inequality, and networks of trust that could inhibit or promote a multilateral project. No matter how it is done, staying close to the experiences of those involved in each project—beneficiaries as well as others—challenges us to do our systemic work effectively and develop and implement projects that demonstrate a clear relationship between research and practice (Tol et al., 2011).

Note

1   The "asylum status" decree is a critical point for any person displaced by war; it is an official status that allows for certain citizen benefits and prevents deportation. Although refugees cannot be forced to return to their home countries in the case of asylum denial, if refused asylum, they can be immediately deported from the host country and sent to a third country.

References

Amarasingam, A., & Dawson, L. (2018). *"I left to be closer to Allah": Learning about foreign fighters from family and friends*. London: Institute for Strategic Dialogue.

Andrimihaja, N. A., Cinyabuguma, M. M., & Devarajan, S. (November 1, 2011) Avoiding the Fragility Trap in Africa. World Bank Policy Research Working Paper No. 5884, Available at SSRN: https://ssrn.com/abstract=1961471

Cape Town Principles and Best Practices (1997). *On the prevention of recruitment of children into the armed forces and on demobilisation and social integration of child soldiers in Africa*. Cape Town, South Africa: UNICEF.

Charlés, L. L. (2015). Scaling up family therapy in fragile, conflict-affected states. *Family Process, 54* (3), 545–558.

Mollica, R. F., Caspi-Yavin, Y., Bollini, P., Truong, T., Tor, S., & Lavelle, J. (1992). The Harvard Trauma Questionnaire: Validating a cross-cultural instrument for measuring torture, trauma, and posttraumatic stress disorder in Indochinese refugees. *Journal of Nervous and Mental Disease, 180* (2), 111–116.

Charlés, L. (2012). Producing evidence of a miracle: Exemplars of therapy conversation with a survivor of torture. Family Process, 51, 25–42.

Monforte, T. (2007). Razing child soldiers. *Alif: Journal of Comparative Poetics, 27*,169–208.

Phama, P. N., Vincka, P., & Weinstein, H. M. (2010). Human rights, transitional justice, public health and social reconstruction. *Social Science and Medicine, 70,* 98–105.

Saul, J., & Bava, S. (September, 2008). Implementing collective approaches to massive trauma/loss in Western contexts: Implications for recovery, peacebuilding and development. *The Trauma, Development and Peacebuilding Conference,* New Delhi, India.

Song, S., Tol, W., & de Jong, J. (2014). Indero: Intergenerational trauma and resilience between Burundian former child soldiers and their children. *Family Process, 53* (2), 239–51.

Spradley, J. P. (1979). *The ethnographic interview.* New York: Holt, Rinehart and Winston.

Tol, W. A., Patel, V., Tomlinson, M., Baingana, F., Galappatti, A., Panter-Brick, C., Silove, D., Sondorp, E., Wessells, M., & van Ommeren, M. (2011). Research priorities for mental health and psychosocial support in humanitarian settings. *Lancet, 8* (9).

Tilly, C. (2002). *Stories, identities, and political change.* New York: Rowman & Littlefield.

Weine, S. (2020). *Disengaging from violent extremism. Kickoff for USIP initiative on violent extremist disengagement and reconciliation.* U.S. Institute for Peace. Accessed from: www.usip.org/events/disengaging-violent-extremism

Weine, S. M. (2011). Developing preventive mental health interventions for refugee families in resettlement. Family Process, 50, 410–430.

Weine S., Ware, N., & Klebic A. (2004). Converting cultural capital among teen refugees and their families from Bosnia-Herzegovina. *Psychiatric Services, 55* (8), 923–927.

8

BARGAINING FOR THE FUTURE

Family Identity and State-Citizen Relational Process in Post-War Kosovo

When I texted my friends that I was going to Gračanica this morning, they asked me: Who is Gračanica? Here, in Gračanica, it is like I am in another country. Everything is Serbian. First and last—Serbian. The cab ride from Pristina only takes 10 minutes! As long as it takes to go to Cambridge from Boston. But it as different as entering Canada from Vermont. Just like my colleagues in Pristina, these folks did not ask to be in the war. They feel as tied to their ethnic identity as anyone. This trip is very disconcerting. In Pristina, it seems as if there is no acknowledgement of the people here, the place. Like it doesn't exist. It is not part of the consciousness of the country.

In 2017, I left my home in Massachusetts to embark on a Fulbright Global Scholar Award, a regional grant funded by the U.S. Department of State and the Council for International Exchange of Scholars (CIES). My first Fulbright had been in Sri Lanka, the year after its civil war ended. This time, 8 years later, I would be returning to Sri Lanka but also, to Kosovo. As a multi-country, trans-regional award, the Fulbright Global Scholar award was an incredible research luxury. I was able to spend the next year of my life traveling between the two regions of the world, exploring how each country's state structures and international partnerships support (or subvert) strategies of scaling up mental health services for families.

In post-conflict and fragile states, health infrastructure, including mental health and psychosocial support, may be challenged at best, or at worst, nonexistent. I had already spent many years traveling to work in Sri Lanka, and had also worked for over a decade in different projects with colleagues in Kosovo. Fortunately, situations in both Kosovo and Sri Lanka were such that when I arrived for my Fulbright Global, institutional capacity had increased, and political violence or continuing violence after the previous conflict had decreased.

Further, each country had a better developed health structure, in which they had been developing capacity in the years since the war. In this research project, I wanted to analyze the efficiency and utility of MHPSS family systems service delivery in the country. I wanted to analyze Tilly's (2002) questions about networks of trust, and the greater social good that may come from increased family and community health and well-being after war. Tilly was the new set of eyes I took with me.

In post-conflict states, the challenges to delivering family-focused mental health and psychosocial support (MHPSS) projects can be better understood by examining how each country's state structures and international partnerships support MPHSS strategies of scaling up, which focuses on enhancing professionals' skill mix and skill set, and task-shifting across health care professions to competently deliver services to families after war. However, in some conflict affected states, because the nature of the relationship between the state and its citizens is compromised, it is not safe to pay attention to these questions. Posing them inherently raises a potential challenge to the status quo, which in some states, cannot be breached safely. Kosovo and Sri Lanka were enjoying increasing democratic consolidation, and conditions that I felt at the time would allow me to conduct such research openly and independently, alongside my colleagues in each country.

The trip to Gračanica inspired many questions and thoughts for my field notebook.

On the way home from Gračanica, the taxi driver talked an age-old story of prejudice: "The Albanians have too many kids. You see, all around, kids.... Serbians, we have one or two." I watched the people walking outside through my window, wanting to ignore him but finding him hard to ignore, too. "Before, Yugoslavia was great, lots of work, I was phone repair guy, here, Belgrade, Montenegro, Sarajevo...but now, nothing! No work!' Democracia!'... It's good for you, but for us? We are a state in transition, from socialist to capitalist. We are a persecuted minority." I heard him, but I had tuned him out when he said Albanians had too many kids. Later, I WhatsApped my diplomat friend Nina, and felt so validated when she reminded me about "The cleavages of history." Yes. Exactly.

For this Serbian taxi driver, having lived in Gračanica, in Kosovo, the former Yugoslavia, what did it mean to be a citizen of one state, yet hold his primary national identity with another state? When his identity as a citizen is with a neighboring state, which doesn't officially recognize the existence of the actual country he is living in? Leaving Gračanica, I realized I needed to understand much better the role of Belgrade in Kosovo. I didn't seem to know how to explain it to myself.

When I told my colleagues in Pristina how I felt traumatized by Gračanica, and what I'd learned after (i.e. Ch. 35 and the #SAA), one said to me: "I can't stop to think about it. If I stop, I won't be able to do anything." For them, making time for reflection could leave them feeling as sad as me. Or worse—hopeless. And then what? I remember hearing that in Libya, too. Yet the busy-ness I'd seen in Tripoli felt to me that it had a purpose. I didn't feel then that the Libyans were avoiding reflection.

However, it was very early days in Libya when I was there. Kosovo had many years to try to repurpose their productivity; Libya is a very different story today than in the heady days of the post-revolution. Both countries are facing deep economic challenges. Neither is as productive, in economics terms anyway, as they used to be. The productivity curve is down in Kosovo. Trepça, the mine in Mitrovica, used to be ⅓ of Kosovo GNP. Josip Tito declared Kosovo an autonomous province in 1974; back then, Kosovars enjoyed autonomy. Now, they enjoy independence as a sovereign state.

Perhaps it is from my training and experience as a qualitative researcher, but when I don't understand something, instead of avoiding the confusion it might bring, I tend to dive further into it. So, five days after my trip to Gračanica, I traveled to Mitrovica, the heart of the Serbian minority population in Kosovo. Mitrovica is a brief 45-minute drive from Pristina. Yet I had never been to the town, despite my many trips to Kosovo. Nor had I met anyone who was from there. "The conflict in Kosovo has had a considerable impact on internal movements, with around 30% of those displaced by the war moving within Kosovo, mainly to urban areas" (Muçaj, 2017).

I actually went many times to Mitrovica, to find out what its absence in Pristina was exactly all about. That is just like me; step right into the confusion in order to sort it all out. There is something like that in family therapy, too. I figure out patterns in the system more clearly by allowing myself to just wade into the story. The clarity will come, but you have to be patient, and willing to travel inside the complexity (Charlés, 2019). Hopefully, you will come out the other side with some new eyes, and perhaps a useful way to see the things you are looking at.

Mitrovica: Caught in Time

There were two or three NGOs in Mitrovica that I had contacted for a visit, after being given their names by staff at the U.S. Embassy, where I'd had a briefing upon my arrival in Pristina. Each of the NGOs was doing very interesting work with families. However, the closer I got to Mitrovica, the more of a focus everything seemed to take on the bridge that divides the town. Indeed, two of the NGOs I wanted to talk to were on the other side of the bridge. The Mitrovica bridge is quite plain and small, yet its complex symbolism is a perfect metaphor for my short time across this region of the Balkans.

During a visit to the Mitrovica bridge in early 2017, High Representative of the European Union (EU) for Foreign Affairs and Security Policy Federica Mogherini described it as "a symbol of the fractures, the wars and the pain marking the history of the Balkans in the last 25 years." But, she added, the bridge can now be turned into "a symbol of dialogue, reconciliation, hope." Mogherini, as High Representative of the EU Foreign

Affairs, exemplifies one of the key regional partners that are so critical in post-conflict Kosovo.

In post-conflict states, during the transition from war to peace, many factors relevant to reconstruction shape everyday family life in the country, as much as they shape and are shaped by foreign policy. The Mitrovica bridge symbolizes a division in the town, in the country, and in the region. It represents many things relevant to foreign policy, trade, and rule of law. However, it is also, quite literally and simply, a bridge. Citizens cross it daily and repeatedly—to get to their jobs, to buy bread or household goods, or to go to school or university. Such is the double life of families living in post-conflict states. The past and the present, war and post-war, compete constantly for your attention.

The violent break-up of the former state of Yugoslavia resulted in the emergence of the new sovereign state of Kosovo in 2008. I was at ease in Kosovo; I had remained in contact with my colleagues over the years, consulting on cases and providing supervision support. Nevertheless, it seemed to me at that moment that my knowledge of the country was quite limited—even given all the time I'd spent immersing in it. How could I find other ways to understand state capacity or incapacity, to address and promote MHPSS in the country?

Observations by the Special Rapporteur, Mr. Pablo de Greiff, on the promotion of truth, justice, reparation and guarantees of non-recurrence, on the conclusion of his 2018 visit to Sri Lanka, noted something that is also quite relevant for Kosovo and the context I found myself in there during my fieldwork:

> In low trust contexts, typical in the aftermath of large-scale violations, where trust between citizens, among groups, and between them and state institutions has been shattered, policies meant to increase understanding about the conditions that led to the violations, to make narrow and reliable attributions of responsibility, offer diverse forms of reparation to victims so as to contribute to their being able to resume at least part of their lives with an increased sense of wellbeing, and to reform institutions so that the violations do not happen again.
>
> (United Nations Office of the High Commissioner of Human Rights, 2018)

de Grieff further noted:

> Since one of the aims of transitional justice is to foster trust (among individuals, between communities, and among them and state institutions), but of course transitional justice initiatives do not operate in a vacuum, other measures that have the potential to either foster or undermine the achievement of that aim need to be carefully considered.
>
> (OHCHR, 2018)

The UN Secretary General's (2004) definition of transitional justice is "the full range of processes and mechanisms associated with a society's attempts to come to terms with a legacy of large-scale past abuses in order to ensure accountability, serve justice and achieve reconciliation." Attempts to come to terms with that legacy often include a very important issue: Memorialization. As de Grieff put it, "Memorialization can have a reparative effect provided that it is even-handed and not used by anybody as part of a zero-sum game in which the basic task is to reaffirm a single-sided narrative" (OHCHR, 2018).

In Kosovo, I decided to focus my efforts on understanding the legacies of the war on areas outside the capital; numerous massacres had taken place outside Pristina during both Balkan wars, but I had had very little exposure to life outside Pristina. In addition to Gračanica and Mitrovica, I traveled to many other villages. Each one I went to, I'd learn about yet another massacre in a different place, giving me yet another destination outside Pristina.

When I told Suhail that I had been to the town of Krush e Madhe, he told me: "They died like B-I-T-C-H-E-S there!!" I'd met Suhail a few weeks' earlier, and we often ran into each other during my walks across the village where he lived. He was fluent in English, Spanish, and German, and was an entrepreneur travel guide for this reason. Like so many others his age, he was also trying very hard to leave the country and find better work in Europe. Animated and intelligent, I felt he was also quite transparent and honest with me about his views. I was still surprised to hear him speak with such vehemence about

Krush e Madhe, but not surprised that he chose to spell out the curse word; he was a devout Muslim.

"You know what I mean?" Suhail asked. To my reply of "No," Suhail continued his story. "They were taken in a room and all shot; they were found covered and hiding. One woman survived. They all fell dead on top of her. It's the village with the largest population of women in Kosovo."

Stories like this, unexpected and powerful, were the reasons I had traveled to the out of the way places. Young people's stories, particularly in Kosovo, were especially powerful. And they could be found anywhere, if you were willing to spend the time. I could see from my trips to Mitrovica, and in particular, North Mitrovica, where I'd been cautioned against visiting, how much more complex my understandings needed to be to accommodate with any clarity the current context in Kosovo.

Srebreniça

After working with my colleagues over several weeks in Kosovo, and encountering more questions about the war than answers, I decided to visit Srebreniça, in Bosnia and Herzogovina (BiH). The war in Kosovo is part of a complex Balkan history and one of several wars in the Balkans after the fall of Yugoslavia. Srebreniça, a neighbor to Pristina, yet very hard to reach from Pristina, was important for me to visit. The memorial exhibits were powerful—the old Dutchbat Headquarters brought with it the deep grief and graphic shock I felt when I visited Auschwitz. The cemetery was reminiscent for me of Arlington National Cemetery in Virginia.

My colleagues in the Balkans, some of whom have managed to go to Srebreniça, are a mixture of Albanians, Bosnians, Kosovars, and Serbians. Going to Srebreniça, and then talking about it with others in the region, was an opportunity for me to learn more about what citizens of the Balkans think of what has happened since the wars. For one man, a survivor of the Srebreniça death march, Srebreniça is his home—he will never leave it, no matter the ongoing divisions. I admired that. For another, a survivor of the siege of Sarajevo, it's a sad, desolate, place that gives him a headache. I respected him for his honesty. For another, Srebreniça is an important place to bring people, to remember, and for her, to talk about with outsiders. As one of the outsiders, I felt honored to be in her company. Yet another, a Bosnian, only in her 20s, told me she has come three times here, because, she says, it's a duty to come, as citizens. I thought that was amazing. I felt as if it was my duty, too.

"The best way to shape the future is to work in the direction of the future" —Claudio Grossman

Back in Pristina, after Srebreniça, I had to figure out how to work in the present moment, but also, with a mind's eye toward the future. Along with my program partners from the Kosovo Association for Family Therapy, University of Mitrovica, and the University Clinical Center in Pristina, we held a roundtable discussion at a local hotel, themed "Trauma and Family: Strengthening Systems Across Communities After War." The participants, from more than a dozen local NGOs and International Organizations, challenged all of us to think about the future—in balance with and alongside the past—for families in Kosovo and across the Balkans.

One critical aspect to think about is psychosocial support. Indeed, this had been one of the key findings of the Consultation Task Force in Sri Lanka (2016).

Yet another overarching consideration that comes out of the consultation process is the need for psychosocial considerations to be factored into the design and operations of transitional justice mechanisms, in particular, restorative psychosocial support and assistance to those affected, be they civilians or combatants across all ethnic divides.

(Consultation Task Force, 2016, p. 96)

I noticed that young people in the roundtable in Pristina, in particular, seemed especially frustrated with the pace of change. I saw this in North Mitrovica, too. They have the least to lose by speaking out, and so it was often their voices I heard. At the same time, it is young people who have such potential for the return of all investments made in their country's future. I invited psychosocial professionals I'd met in North Mitrovica, and consulted with my colleagues in Pristina about how their collabor-ation might work. At the roundtable, I felt their presence in the room—at the very least, the open question of their absence.

Prekaz

I learned so much in Kosovo from the time I spent with local people, and especially, young persons—as it seems they all are in Kosovo, the youngest country in Europe. I asked one of these young people, Jetmir, who I met in Prizren, if I could pay him to drive me to Prekaz, so that I could visit the memorial there. It is in the heart of the country, and not easy to access without a car, which I didn't have. We had become friends over the past few weeks I'd spent in his city; he had never been to Prekaz, so this would also give him an opportunity to see the memorial site. He had a vehicle, and a day off in the next week. As we sat in the café planning our trip, I noticed an old calendar on the wall behind the cash register, with a picture of the Clintons on it, from a visit they had made to a refugee camp in Macedonia in 1999. "We do not forget" was hand-written on the side.

Baç, U Kry! A large sign into the entrance cries out, with a black and white drawing of a man in a traditional Kosovar garb. "Brother, we did it!" my friend Jetmir translated. The outdoor museum has a red colored series of stones, forming a very long line as if a road, leading to the bullet-casing mural profile of Adem Jashari, and spread out to all the graves. It's meant to represent blood. The red line goes from the houses to the graves. A river of blood.

The memorial complex is just as finely tuned as Srebreniça's. The destroyed home is left, with evidence of the mortars and gunfire and destruction to the point of bomb blasts, fanning out to reveal pockmarked shell damage and the black soot of gunpowder. You walk around, and you get an absolute sense of how besieged they were. You see the damage from all sides, around the entire complex, not ever just one side. The siege went on for three days. We spent hours there—from eleven to three o'clock. Twice as long as we'd planned. It went by quickly.

The area surrounding the houses was full of hills on all sides, with deep green meadows full of flowers, under a bright sky, with the scent of nature, pasture, and air. It is a beautiful place, and one wonders, or rather, stops wondering, why someone would defend such a peaceful, natural land.

As we drove away from Prekaz, Jetmir at the wheel, I was thinking about the guards who had rushed to meet us each time we stopped to see the name on a grave. We were the only visitors at first; a few arrived after us. However, as in so many parts of rural Kosovo, I felt I had the place to myself. I remember what the guide had said to us at the museum, and how quiet it all was.

As a U.S. citizen, I often have extra attention on me when I travel, and in Kosovo, that was particularly so. The guide at the museum had described the exhibits, and when we were done, he chose a moment to thank me for visiting. I looked at Jetmir, who was watching the guide so very closely as he spoke to me. I remembered that it was Jetmir's first time, here, too. He had already worked in Belgium and Switzerland, but had never been to Prekaz. The guide said to me: "I thank you a citizen of the U.S., to all the U.S. people, for your efforts to help us in the war. Thank you to the United States." He said this to me as if I was a diplomat, as if I was representing an entire country. I was only a visitor, but I had heard words like this many times in Kosovo. This time, I was at a loss for words. The guide's comments were so gracious. Yet, it was Jetmir's face, brimming with tears, that silenced me.

References

Charlés, L. (2017) From Boston to the Balkans: My Fulbright Global Scholar Award in postwar regions of the world. *Council for International Exchange of Scholars (CIES)*, https://www.cies.org/article/boston-balkans-my-fulbright-global-scholar-award-postwar-regions-world

Charlés, L. (2018a). Hearing firsthand: Exploring Sri Lanka on my Fulbright Global Scholar Award. *Council for International Exchange of Scholars (CIES)*, https://www.cies.org/article/hearing-firsthand-exploring-sri-lanka-my-fulbright-global-scholar-award

Charlés, L. (2018b). Everything is dangerous: Crossing borders in brief sex therapy. In S. Green & D. Flemons (Eds.), *Quickies, 3rd edition* (pp. 216–232). New York: Norton.

Charlés, L. (2019). My global team of family therapy consultants: Seven commandments of my method. In L. Charlés & T. Nelson's (Eds.), Family therapy supervision in extraordinary settings: Illustrations of systemic approaches in everyday clinical work (pp.128–137). London: Routledge.

Consultation Task Force on Reconciliation Mechanisms (November 17, 2016) *Final report of the Consultation Task Force on reconciliation mechanisms, Volume I.*

Muçaj, D. (2017). Use of illicit drugs among young adults in post-conflict society Kosovo 2002-2013. Health in Humanitarian Crisis Centre seminar, London School of Hygiene and Tropical Medicine. Retrieved from https://www.mhinnovation.net/use-illicit-drugs-among-young-adults-post-conflict-society-kosovo-2002-2013

United Nations Human Rights Office of the High Commissioner of Human Rights (April 11, 2018). Observations by the Special Rapporteur on the promotion of truth, justice, reparation and guarantees of non-recurrence, Mr. Pablo de Greiff, on the conclusion of his recent visit to Sri Lanka [Press release]. Accessed at: www.ohchr.org/EN/NewsEvents/Pages/DisplayNews.aspx?NewsID=15820&LangID=E

UN Secretary General (August 23, 2004). *The rule of law and transitional justice in post-conflict societies.* UN Doc. S/2004/616, paragraph 8. Accessed at: www.securitycouncilreport.org/atf/cf/%7B65BFCF9B-6D27-4E9C-8CD3-CF6E4FF96FF9%7D/PCS%20S%202004%20616.pdf

Tilly, C. (2002). *Stories, identities, and political change.* New York: Rowman & Littlefield.

9

WHO KEEPS THE PEACE AND WHO MAKES THE PEACE?

How Family and Community Engagement
Is Used to Strengthen Reconciliation and
Transitional Justice Mechanisms in Sri Lanka

According to Paul Salem (1993), an assumption exists that it is solely physical violence—killing, and death—that is the most abhorrent of all human rights atrocities. Death and physical violence, rather than grief or sorrow after violence, often merits the most attention, and the immediate intervention. In his critique of this focus on physical violence, Salem asks, "Is physical pain indeed more painful than non-physical pain? Is a serious flesh wound worse than a serious injustice?"

(Salem, 1993, p. 364, as cited in Charlés, 2015)

Snow started to fall as I looked out the window of my airplane leaving Kosovo, where I had spent six weeks on a Fulbright Global Scholar award, analyzing post conflict mechanisms that support family psychosocial health. I was feeling overwhelmed, but that was to be expected in the middle of an intense research project. What I was also feeling was: Gratitude. As we sat on the tarmac, watching the storm that forced our delay, I felt so lucky to have had such a powerful and instructive time in Kosovo. I had witnessed so many deep changes unfolding in real time, issues to do with identity and Kosovo's challenges with reconciliation. I wondered if it would be similar in Sri Lanka, where I was headed next. Would the issues be the same in their own post-war transition? How would it be different?

Reconciliation Efforts Are Relational Processes

Reconciliation efforts in post-conflict societies are focused on strengthening both institutional reforms and interpersonal processes, each of which is seen as a way to rebuild and repair relationships following armed conflict. In particular, relationships and relational process are seen as key to atrocity prevention and the recurrence of conflict. That is, conflict prevention literature highlights relationship building, community engagement, and grassroots, citizen-based movements in post conflict states as critical to eroding the damage of grievances, the violent conflict and the trauma of war.

However, it seems to me that relational phenomena are typically the "black box" of atrocity and conflict prevention literature. For example, issues labelled as "trust"; "empathy"; and "respect" are key indicators used in the extant literature. However, they are not defined relationally— and often, not defined at all. The end of a separatist war or violent conflict in a country can leave lingering questions about what comes after. What is the narrative of reconciliation and the how does that inform the processes of post-conflict reconstruction?

It is a challenge to make relational processes something measurable, deliverable, and feasible in transitional justice research. Systemic family therapy scholars are quite familiar with this challenge. It is a familiar challenge for transitional justice researchers as well, perhaps. In the extant research, I have found little specific information or in-depth descriptions of the interactional processes by which previously warring groups go about transforming their relationships after conflict. This must change if relational process is to be taken seriously as a useful concept in the discourse on peacebuilding.

Welcome Back to Sri Lanka!

We arrived in Sri Lanka the next afternoon, and, as I started up my phone in the taxi en route to Colombo, I was back in research mode: A text arrived from my colleague at the University of Colombo, who wrote: "There is a Symposium on Development and Social Science Research at the University; come if you can." Of course, I went. The presentations focused on so many interesting things relevant to my project, with a clear lens on the economic, social, and political aftermath of the war, all over this country of 23 million people. Sri Lanka is in the midst of designing, discussing and implementing what everyone I talked to referred to as "TJ": Transitional Justice.

Since my first Fulbright in Sri Lanka in 2010, when I lectured and conducted research in Colombo, I had collaborated many times with Sri Lankan scholars and practitioners. These colleagues are absolute experts on issues of community engagement and public mental health in post-war settings. However, despite the many trips to Sri Lanka and collaborations in between then and now, I'd never been beyond Vavuniya, which is somewhat in the center of the island. I'd attempted to go to the northern town of Jaffna before; however, at that time, foreigners were not allowed to visit.

Jaffna is quite a lengthy road trip from Colombo—8 hours by car, and 10 hours by train. There is no easy way to get there, but it is certainly worth the trip—if only for the arrival, itself a profound experience. I will never forget the expanse of land and palms; the air; the shift in how the land looked from what had come before. I had traveled to the North of Sri Lanka with some colleagues working on psychosocial support and transitional justice mechanisms for families after the war. I had agreed to conduct a training, alongside them, for a set of psychosocial workers located in the north of the country.

Accessing Places and People Inaccessible during the War

Transitional justice and reconciliation, after war, is contextual like everything else. How it looks in each place is so highly dependent on everything. There are common processes, and patterns, which are familiar to me as a systems thinker. It did not escape my notice that in the current work I was doing, a high priority emerged that surprised me—inasmuch as it feels so obvious in hindsight. That was: Visiting places and peoples that had not been easily accessible during the war—and only slightly more so, post-war.

After our training in the Northern province, my team in Sri Lanka dropped me off at Kilinochchi, another town that is a bit further north from Vavuniya. Kilinochchi was once the capital city of the LTTE, the Liberation Tigers of Tamil Eelam, who had waged a decades long civil war inside Sri Lanka. "Killi," as it was referred to amongst absolutely everyone—not only those who had trouble pronouncing the full name of Kilinochchi—was a fascinating place on its own. The scars of the war were everywhere. This, and its distance from Colombo, easily made it seem like a very far-off, strange, and elusive destination.

For the group I was traveling with, Killi was simply a practical junction. One of the counsellors had her family there; we were dropping her off to have a short visit with her loved ones. Thanks to that, I was able to get a drop-off, too. Killi was not Jaffna, but it was close enough, and all of us deemed it was very doable for me to get there on my own the next morning. So that was the plan, and it seemed very good. I remember feeling grateful to be part of this group, to be on the road with them. It was dark night outside, and I remember the ride and the company as lovely, all of us chatting about the road trip and our reflections about the training we had just completed.

I spent the night in Killi in a lovely small auberge. My room had air conditioning and hot, running water—notable because there is certainly a distinction between these rooms and the people (often foreigners, but not always) who take them. My NGO counterpart had made sure I had this room, though I was only staying overnight to sleep. I have lived and worked so many places with no electricity nor plumbing—much less a/c or hot, running water—so I don't see myself as one of those "difficult foreigners" who cannot deal. But who knows? Perhaps I *am* one of those difficult foreigners. We are always the last ones to know how we are perceived—something I've learned over and over again in my years of this consulting work.

Nevertheless—what was on my mind wasn't the a/c or the hot water. I hadn't eaten since lunch, and my colleague, the lead psychologist in the NGO, someone I've known a few years, suggested the *exact* meal I should choose to eat at the hotel. I love the spicy heat of Sri Lankan food—we make it all the time at home, with spices we hoard every time we travel to the island, and with the guidance of a lovely "cookery book" that we bought on our first trip. I grew up in Texas and I consider myself an expert taster when it comes to heat in my meals. My NGO colleague knew this very well, and I delighted in her recommendations. Now I was able to receive them beyond the urban scape of Colombo.

My colleague promised me the food would be good at the auberge. It was. One of the staff walked the meal she recommended to my room a couple of hours after I'd ordered it (it seemed the cook was away when I arrived). He brought it to my room so I wouldn't have to eat in the outdoor dining area in the midst of the rain storm. During the night, I heard a small dog sleeping outside my door, perhaps to escape the rain. Fleas on his coat also came inside my room to warm themselves, but I was already away and gone the next morning before I had time to reflect on this pleasant evening in Killi—my first, but fortunately, not my last.

The next day, with the help of my NGO friends' office tuk-tuk, I caught a bus to Jaffna. The bus ride would be short, and easy, so I wasn't worried, even though I have no Sinhala or Tamil, and no one I met in Killi had English. We were clearly in Tamil language areas now, though. I'd spent so much time in Sinhala language areas of the country it really was a vivid change to feel the stark difference in language. I loved it. I knew many of my Sinhala colleagues would love to be here with me, too. Few of them had had time to explore the North of their country, and because of the lengthy war, knew very little about it. I knew I was very lucky.

While the bus traversed all kinds of back roads, lurching from tiny townlet to townlet assertively looking for passengers, I had a blast people-watching, listening to the language shift abruptly to Tamil from Sinhala, and gazing open-mouthed at the beautiful landscape. Shortly after the bus trip started, I caught a glimpse of Killi's destroyed water tank from the war. I had heard of this, of course—but I'd never expected to see it. We had passed it at night, in the dark, during our road trip. We'd also passed the famous Government of Sri Lanka memorial in Kilinochchi. A piece of concrete slab, standing upright, with a piece of ordnance in its center. On the top of the slab was a lotus flower, also in concrete. Last night, I couldn't get a glimpse of it save for the spotlights all around it, which overwhelmed the darkness. This morning, I saw both the memorial and the destroyed water tank.

Memorialization and the State-Citizen Relationship After War

War and conflict transform a nation, and its people. I had seen so much of that in my own consultation work in conflict affected countries, and certainly, in my home country of the U.S. However, after spending time in the Balkans and now Sri Lanka, I was struck by how often memorials of any kind about the fighting also concomitantly told the story about what the country was focused on post war. Its identity, its relationship with its citizens, with its neighbors, and of course, within the international community (Charlés, 2018a).

One of the first things that seems to suffer during conflict is institutions of knowledge, such as libraries. If you want to destroy a people, destroy their libraries, their archives, their history. And so, it was in the beautiful Jaffna library—burned to the ground right before the war and now rebuilt—where I found the people, working so hard to re-engage with their history, and their future. I didn't know anyone in Jaffna, not directly. I wasn't sure how I would go about finding what I wanted. Like the qualitative researcher I am, I didn't know what I needed to ask until I was in the field. Only then did the questions become clearer.

"We are a defeated people," Dharam told me, my second day in Jaffna. I had spent the day at the Jaffna library. The library was full of students, local people reading the newspapers, scholars working to tell stories of the Tamil peoples' experience, and, to my surprise, piles of shoes at the front door. Libraries are such sacred places, but I'd never seen shoes at the steps of the library to show it.

Dharam was kind to me, and willing to share, over a cup of tea each day I spent in Jaffna, his experience during war, as well as his impressions of what it was like in Jaffna today. As I'd heard many times in Kosovo, a country of 2 million compared to Lanka's 23 million, "The biggest problem is unemployment for young people." This commonality shared by the two countries was as striking to me as the differences. In addition to the issues with youth unemployment, each country has deeply powerful narratives of victory and defeat.

At the dinner table one night, with a colleague visiting from another post-war country, we talked about how unusual it seemed to him that Sri Lanka, in his view, was only now talking about reconciliation—ten years after the war's end. Talking about reconciliation is a process of dialogue that takes place between people, over an extended period of time. Dialogue inside a state, between states, is of course relational. Because these relationships change over time, the dialogue, of course, changes over time. It can seem like it has started overnight, but that is rarely the case.

At the end of the war, in Sri Lanka, dialogue was about "victory" over terrorists. At the time of my Fulbright Global in 2017 and 2018, it was about "TJ," and perhaps, accompanying war widows to the newly established Office of Missing Persons (OMP). Only then did it seem safe in Sri Lanka to speak overtly about reparations of post-war, such as the recovery of land, the search for justice, and truth. In Kosovo, the dialogue is at a much different place along the continuum.

In the Republic of Kosovo, they were just beginning to approve in Parliament their mechanism of truth and reconciliation when I was there. I think this is somewhat ahead of RKS civil society, who does not seem to be having that category of discourse. In Sri Lanka, it seems to be the opposite—civil society is ahead of state actors in the discourse of reconciliation.

Each country faces international pressures as well as internal, domestic ones. For Sri Lanka, it is pressure from the UN about its human rights record; for Kosovo, it is pressure from the EU about its relationship with Serbia. Both sets of pressures have dramatic implications for each country's trade, labor and employment, international and regional status, and foreign direct investment.

Returning to a Place and Seeing It for the First Time

I have lost count of the number of times I have traveled and worked in Sri Lanka. Even when I am not there, in one way or another, Sri Lanka is always with me. The country inspires my professional curiosities in such robust ways. Each effort I make to address a research curiosity results in other questions and so, I've read so much work by and for Sri Lankans, who are a prolific set of folks. In fact, if you walked over to my bookcase, you'd find four shelves of books about Sri Lanka—its history as an island, the war, the aftermath, and non-fiction books, too. I felt I had absorbed Sri Lanka. But, in the end, none of that really had foretold what I was about to experience.

In going to Jaffna, I felt like I was seeing Sri Lanka for the first time. Many of my Colombo colleagues who have been to Jaffna since the war had told me of a similar sensation. Going there was as if they were seeing a country they did not know. The people I met in Jaffna also reminded me of other communities I've worked in where the end of war has opened them up to a different vision and a different story of who they are.

The stories about the war in Jaffna were different than the ones I'd heard in Colombo. For example, the war injuries I had heard or read about were now told to me firsthand, not second- nor third-, as before. The changes in livelihoods since the end of the war I did not need to read about; they were there, right in front of me. The urbanization of Jaffnatown, as people moved away from more rural areas, was first pointed out to me by Dharam, the local scholar who sat with me for hours sharing his observations. The shift in livelihoods after the war was reminiscent of Kosovo; both were experiencing this phenomenon.

Stories of the war were everywhere. Everyone I met had lived through it in one way or another, as a resident or as someone newly returned from exile. On this trip, it was the Jaffna library where I began to hear such stories. The experiences I had only brought more questions.

Focusing on Families and their Meaningful Engagement in Transitional Justice Mechanisms

Families are part of the continuum of citizenry, alongside individuals and communities, worthy of examination and critical to the relationship building that is needed in transitional justice mechanisms. Clearly, increasing resiliency of a state requires strengthened community engagement and robust state-citizen phenomena on the ground. This is particularly so in conflict-affected states, as a strengthened community can contribute to the social determinants of individual and family health, as well as increased productivity, employment, and economic growth.

Lonergan (2017) noted that:

> [F]ostering the interpersonal process required to build peaceful relationships and strengthen meaningful dialogue between formerly conflicting groups is a serious challenge, as each group preserves competing stories about the conflict and their identity in relation to it.

Families are key to how individual identity is constructed. They are both a risk and a protective factor for individuals (Walsh, 2016), and not to be excluded from understanding relationships and relational process in peacebuilding and conflict prevention. Families really are "peacebuilding from below," particularly in conflict-affected states, where they are challenged to transform their identities from war to post-war, and interact within the frame of multiple narratives about peace and security and reconciliation.

Yet, the extant literature does not take a systemic approach to understanding relationship and relational process of families and communities in post-war settings. Nor does it examine how families and their meaningful engagement is incorporated as an environmental condition in peacebuilding. There are no tools nor methods in conflict prevention and transitional justice that focus on families, or family process.

Family therapy scholars are quite skilled at research methods and clinical praxis that can sophisticatedly address how families function and, also, what helps them thrive. We know how to conduct research with families to elicit their understanding about their processes. Our field can influence transitional justice policy by bringing more comprehensive understanding of how states engage families and communities to strengthen their efforts at "peacebuilding from below." In particular, we can say something about what inhibits family engagement, and what promotes it. Specifically, family therapy scholars can analyze: (1). Civil society-based community dialogues that bring families together on issues of memorialization; (2). Family-based interventions in postwar settings, including mental health and psychosocial support relevant to sequelae of war related violence and narratives about war trauma; (3). The specific transitional justice mechanisms co-occurring in each state and how state and civil society—including families—are engaged in in the process of community building and state strengthening.

Focusing on how families are included (or not) in peacebuilding and transitional justice in conflict-affected regions can more directly address the gap in knowledge and scholarship about the micro-relational processes so critical to promoting transitional justice efforts. A focus on inclusive family engagement can also bring some new questions and ideas to policy relevance in conflict prevention research and peacebuilding. It can center our attention on how informal structures and ordinary people contribute to making and keeping the peace, when all obstacles seem to prevent it. A focus on families can get to the heart of how identity is shaped and transformed in conflict-affected states. It is an underrepresented area in conflict prevention literature. It has great potential to contribute to the outcomes, design, and the long-term sustainability and durability of peace processes.

References

Charlés, L. (28 June, 2018a). *Looking back, looking ahead: Post transitional justice in Kosovo and its relevance in relation to Sri Lanka: Memorialization, identity, family, community*. Colombo, Sri Lanka: The Asia Foundation.

Charlés , L. (2018b). Hearing firsthand: Exploring Sri Lanka on my Fulbright Global Scholar Award. *Council for International Exchange of Scholars (CIES)*, https://www.cies.org/article/hearing-firsthand-exploring-sri-lanka-my-fulbright-global-scholar-award

Charlés, L., & Samarasinghe, G. (October, 2015). *Psychosocial innovation in post war Sri Lanka*. Chagrin Falls, OH: Taos Institute.

Lonergan, K. (2017). Does reconciliation prevent future atrocities? Evaluating practice in Sri Lanka. Peaceworks, 132, 6.

Salem, P. E. (1993). A critique of western conflict resolution from a non-western perspective. *Negotiation Journal*, 9, 361–369.

Walsh, F. (2016). Applying a family resilience framework in training, practice, and research: Mastering the art of the possible. Family Process, 55 (4), 616–632.

10

FRONTLINE RESPONSES TO "BUILD BACK BETTER" DURING TWO PUBLIC HEALTH EMERGENCIES OF INTERNATIONAL CONCERN

Guinea during the 2014 Ebola Virus Disease Epidemic and Massachusetts at the Start of the Covid-19 Pandemic

Dear Shoufi Mafi:

Hello from my 5–star hotel in Conakry. I moved into it about 2 weeks ago from the smaller hotel where all of the non-Guinéen consultants seemed to be staying. The move is mostly for my mental health: This hotel has a gym with two treadmills. Here, I run about 11 k every two days. Running is serious business for my "self-care," as we talked about in Shoufi Mafi. I ran all the time at home in San Antonio, but it is not easy to do during an epidemic. Since I don't drink or smoke to get rid of stress, nor do I work 7 days a week (I work only 6), I had to figure something out. So, I left my hotel, the one where all the foreign expats live. I could immediately feel the difference in my workload and productivity. Not only did I find a treadmill at the new hotel; I also found all the U.S. expats—a huge group from USAID and CDC—whom I had never seen before in Conakry. It seems the expats situate themselves by hotel during EVD? The one I was at before was mostly UN from France, Europe, other countries including Africa, and was very clearly francophone. The crowd at this hotel seems clearly anglophone.

When I began the above missive to my Shoufi Mafi global mental health student group at OLLU (Charlés, 2015a), I had just arrived in West Africa to begin a deployment as a WHO mental health officer, based in the sub-regional coordination center for Ebola Outbreak Response in Conakry, Guinea. A faculty member at the time at a graduate program in Texas, I was taking the summer of 2015 off so as to work in Guinea. Earlier that school year at OLLU, we had started the Shoufi Mafi student group. Our discussions on global mental health and family therapy were on hold for the summer, but at the same time, somewhat heightened by my arrival in Guinea. Everything we had talked about was here, and I wanted to share it with them.

A PHEIC in West Africa: Introducing the International Health Regulations

I arrived in Guinea in 2015, but the Ebola Virus Disease outbreak had actually begun in Guinea in December 2013 and involved transmission in Guinea, Liberia, Nigeria, and Sierra Leone. My arrival in Guinea was eighteen months after the start of the outbreak, and one year after it was declared in July 2014 a PHEIC, a public health emergency of international concern. The term Public Health Emergency of International Concern is defined in the International Health Regulations (2005) as:

an extraordinary event which is determined, as provided in these Regulations:

(1) To constitute a public health risk to other States through the international spread of disease; and
(2) to potentially require a coordinated international response.

This definition implies a situation that carries implications for public health beyond the affected State's national borders; and may require immediate international action.[1]

At the recommendation of health ministers who attended that July 2014 meeting, a response Coordination Centre was to be set up, to be based in Conakry, the capital of Guinea. Within the PHEIC framework, a team was exclusively dedicated to the Ebola emergency response, to assist at the sub-national, national, and international levels. The objective of the Centre was to ensure that partner efforts in supporting governments' response to this outbreak were better coordinated. My presence was a result of that coordinated response.

Terms of Reference for the MHPSS Response

The purpose of my mission was mental health and psychosocial support (MHPSS) implementation and strengthening for the general population and health workers in the context of the outbreak. According to the terms of reference (TOR) of my contract, the expected main achievements for my work were also to include: Stigma reduction; increased MHPSS support for individuals who were confirmed and/or suspected cases of Ebola, including their family members; and increased MHPSS support for health care providers. Reflecting on this TOR as I complete this chapter and this book, I can see it is not unlike the focus of our response today, three months into the Covid-19 pandemic in Massachusetts.

When I arrived in Guinea in 2015, I joined a team that had already worked in the office for several months, in hopes of "Getting to Zero" (Longuépée, 2015). There were hundreds of consultants in the sub-office, of every type of expertise, and we were from all over the world, including many other countries in Africa. I was delighted to meet consultants from Togo, where I had served as a Peace Corps Volunteer, and also some from nearby Senegal, where I hope to travel one day.

As responders to the outbreak, consultants did everything from infection prevention and control to epidemiology; from mental health and psychosocial support to contact tracing; and from laboratory/mobile lab tech to anthropology. This collection of expertise and multilateral country cooperation is part of what came about after the PHEIC declaration. It was an amazing professional experience to work with such a diverse group of professionals, each with deep expertise in their area; it was so reflective of the kind of multidisciplinary response required in emergencies.

The national team I was working with in Guinea most closely had been first responders in other types of MHPSS projects in the country in previous years. They were highly skilled. They were also very kind, young and energetic, curious and super sharp, and, most of all, dedicated. When we weren't on the road, heading to do a training in an affected village, we spent every working day together, inside a din of activity in the Coordination Centre. Once a week, on Fridays, we attended an MHPSS briefing, in which every organization delivering a mental health and psychosocial support response to the outbreak attended. This was one effective way we all could be easily and routinely updated on what was happening with regard to MHPSS in the country.

I moved to Conakry, the capital of Guinea, in mid-May, 2015, and I stayed for three months, the length of a typical contract for a response like this. Many consultants renewed their contracts and stayed much longer; likely I would have done the same had I not a full-time faculty position to return to. Three months in Guinea seemed quite long at the time, or certainly, long enough. However, the last three months in Massachusetts, at the start of Covid-19, just seems like one very long day.

"Getting to Zero"

In Guinea, at the time of my arrival, eighteen months into the epidemic, EVD transmission was continuing at what was considered a high rate: 20–30 cases a week. The number of contacts being followed each week numbered in the thousands, and the amount of international staff involved in the outbreak response in Conakry/Guinea was impressive and overwhelming. Numerous consultants arrived and departed each day; I was constantly meeting new people and saying goodbye to others.

At the time, this constant mobility of teams did not feel disruptive to me, but I am not sure I can tell you why that is. Keeping a ready rotation of consultants mobilized was one sure way to avoid burnout, perhaps. It felt busy, intense, and serious—but there was also a feeling for me of camaraderie, independence, and autonomy. Looking back, I realize now how I arrived at a time that many norms to do with this sort of collective solidarity and team behavior had already become established. Today, I am thinking quite a lot about how beliefs, behavior, and norms are interdependent and mutually reinforcing.

With the exception of the number of consultants, every other number from EVD 2014 in Guinea is completely overwhelmed by the numbers from Covid-19 in Massachusetts. At the time of this writing, Massachusetts has had several days of nearly 200 deaths per day due to Covid-19. Eighteen months into Ebola we in Guinea were all trying to "Get to Zero," i.e., having zero new cases. Less cases equals less deaths. Eventually in Massachusetts we will have the wherewithal to hope beyond hope and talk of "Getting to Zero." But my awareness of that all feels quite thin right now. All I can think is: 200 deaths a day.

In Guinea, I remember feeling thrown into a sea of organized chaos, a little shocked by the intensity and number of people in the response effort. Everyone else seemed to be in the middle of a race, a marathon or ultramarathon, perhaps, somewhat sweaty from the effort, and in a kind of trance, a focused concentration. Whereas I had just arrived to the race. I was disoriented, sluggish from jetlag, and confused by all the strange new norms, including the Purell stands I saw all over Conakry. On my first day, I remember sitting at the big conference table, in one of the working rooms we all used, laptops in front of each of us. I took a picture of the wifi-password, which someone had written in black ink on a large sheet of paper and taped to the wall, so I wouldn't forget it.

Dear Shoufi Mafi,

Although in the outbreak mobility is somewhat restricted, as a team, we move around a lot. A few weeks ago, we went to a region of Guinea called Dubreka. During the outbreak we are required to use WHO vehicles only for transport. That is part of the safety/security re: Ebola protection. We can't use local taxis, even though it sometimes would be faster to do so. It is too risky, re IPC. We also have a 6 p.m. curfew. Yet, I don't feel stuck in place anywhere. I've already traveled to Liberia, for instance. Our team went to Monrovia to join other stakeholders in a mental health and psychosocial support (MHPSS) meeting, to learn and make plans to 'Build Back Better' from the regional effects of the outbreak. The meeting brought together over 75 representatives from the three countries, including members of the ministries of health and social welfare, national and international NGO partners and donor agencies, in addition to WHO MHPSS staff from WHO headquarters, the Afro-regional office and the three WHO country offices.

Our goals for the meeting in Monrovia were: "1. To identify achievements, challenges and lessons learned in relation to the Ebola-related mental health and psychosocial emergency response; 2. To produce a roadmap of mental health system and recovery/development; 3. To identify a minimum response framework for mental health and psychosocial support that can be rolled out in case of similar, future outbreaks in other countries based on the experience of Ebola mental health and psychosocial response in the three countries."

(Pearson, 2015)

Working in International Teams and within an International Organization (I/O)

In Guinea, I am part of a team with two other WHO international consultants. We have more than three working languages between us; French is the only language all three of us are fluent in. The working language of the EVD project in Guinea is French; French is the primary language used amongst Guinea's professional cadre.

The role of WHO in this kind of emergency is not direct, even though it often seems so. As an organ of the United Nations, WHO assists member states to meet their obligations, particularly during an emergency, and has done so since 1948. WHO provides assistance and guidance to countries, through technical expertise and sharing of information, but does so only at the request of member states.

Along these lines, as international staff, our role is to support the national staff. Thus, we work closely with four national consultants, psychiatrists and psychologists who conduct trainings in local languages, not French, but with whom we work and convene in French. In turn, we've discovered we need yet another language to speak and work with the traditional healers, who are often the "first responders" that families turn to when someone becomes symptomatic. Language is just one of the many everyday, ongoing, challenging complexities we must negotiate creatively and proactively during the epidemic.

What my work looks like during the many trainings is this: I am the *responsable*, to use the word we used in Guinea. I often open and close the training with welcoming and encouraging words. This is not typically what I am used to doing in my career as a family therapist. However, it is exactly what I am expected to do here, now. I am a kind of diplomat, deployed during a PHEIC that is Ebola, in West Africa, in French, in a village, in a WHO Coordination Centre.

My host country team does all of the important training work—and they are very good at it. However, they can do so much more with my "official" presence. By virtue of what I represent, I open doors that are otherwise not necessarily open. I would not normally ascribe such importance to that role, but here, during an epidemic, I absolutely must do so. I consult in other ways when my national team ask. This happens most often and particularly when we talk about how to help the community health workers conceptualize family dynamics in their visits to people's homes (Faregh & Charlés, 2017; Faregh, Tounkara & Soumaoro 2019).

I do lots of other things, too. I coordinate my team's travel with the logistics teams and finance teams at the sub-office, which is not as easy as it sounds. Guinea is a cash economy during the outbreak; everything is done with local currency, and I am responsible for carrying the cash to pay all the bills at each training. I carry large blocks of CFA bills, bound together with rubber bands and stuffed in a travel bag that seems heavier each week. I am very happy when the week has ended and I need not worry any further about the security issues of carrying so much cash. But that is part of my job, I think. I worry about that so my team doesn't have to—so they can focus on doing the training they need to do for their countrymen and women. I can focus on making sure everything is paid for, managed, dealt with, so everyone else can focus on Ebola.

Contact Tracing: Supporting ACs

When I arrived in Guinea, the issues were fairly clear with regard to the mental health sequalae of the epidemic, and the areas where capacity could be built. However, the ways to achieve outcomes, the best and most workable solutions, were sometimes less clear. Thus, in addition to our small team, we also coordinate closely with public health professionals in the country to dialogue about the work we are doing. There are meetings, conferences, and trainings every week; there is a focus on the future, the health care system in Guinea, and how a mental health plan can fit into it. However, a constant, clear, and primary focus of our efforts is on supporting health workers in Guinea during the epidemic—in particular, the ACs, *agents communitaires*, or, as we would call them in the U.S., community health workers.

The community health workers are key to stopping transmission of Ebola in Guinea, and they need to be supported to do their work as well as they can for the entire life of the emergency. Villages are at the heart of the outbreak, and their rural location can make the community health workers who work inside them sometimes invisible. Chosen by each village, there are hundreds, thousands, maybe tens of thousands of them in Guinea. This is one asset that Guinea has that so many high-income countries do not.

For example, polio vaccine community health workers are the workforce deployed during Ebola; the infrastructure for contact tracing was there, ready to use. In Massachusetts, we have had to construct this workforce from scratch. Although we are the first state in the U.S. to do so (The Office of Governor Charlie Baker, 2020; Wallace-Wells, 2020), there are real obstacles to overcome, which countries in Africa do not necessarily have. Indeed, "Epidemics are a part of daily life in many developing countries, often accompanying poverty, civil unrest, armed conflicts, or natural disasters" (Victor & Ahmed, 2019, p. 59).

The ACs do health-related work but they are also liaisons to the larger system, and in time of Ebola, this larger system means *surveillance*, or contract tracing, as it is called in English. Contact tracing in Guinea involves finding the people connected to a family or individual exposed to EVD.

The community health workers work six days a week, from sunrise to sunset, and they are on the front lines of the outbreak in a way that we are not, even if we are all here as part of the global response. In our weekly training programs for the community health workers, we focus on psychological first aid, PFA, and also, WHO's mental health Gap Action Program, mhGAP (World Health Organization, 2008)—with a healthy dose of role-plays, depending on what their needs are and on what is happening in their communities. Role-plays are a critical part of our work with them.

The role-plays the ACs show us of their work with families are incredibly sophisticated. The "safe and dignified burial" is so important for the family, and it is the hardest thing for many ACs to deal with. Not every group of community health worker can do this type of sensitive family conversation right now, and we noticed areas with big gaps, which direct and shape our training plans in large and small ways.

For instance, while the community health workers need to be able to help a family understand the need for a safe and dignified burial, they may have a difficulty due to their own discomfort or their own reactions to the family's dynamics and suffering. St. Victor and Ahmed (2019) noted

> Burial practices for the deceased turned out to be one the most important modes of spreading the disease—a common ritual among many religions is washing the dead body with bare hands and spending time with the dead body, which, in the case of Ebola, may be highly contagious.
>
> (p. 60)

Safe, dignified burials as cultural and contextual matters during Ebola were indeed something my team was able to help with in role-plays. In one memorable role-play, the community health workers brought a role-play imam to the family meeting to help the family deal with their spiritual and religious concerns about the burial.

A Layer of Covid-19 Response on Everything

Teamwork during a crisis response of this magnitude is critical to a project's success. It is also so very complicated. In Massachusetts, I do not at the moment work as part of an official —not regional nor internationally deployed—organized response effort. Rather, I am working from home, in my routine professional roles, with a layer of PHEIC Covid-19 on top of them. I find myself contributing to my community in unusual ways, a kind of informal deployment via multiple roles—citizen, health provider, and educator.

Although I am not mobile, except of course virtually via information and communication technologies, ICTs, I very much consider myself part of a "team" during the early days of the pandemic. Perhaps that is because each of my current roles requires me in one way or another to make daily choices about infection prevention, critical to my own safety as well as to the safety of the larger community. I think about my team as my family, my colleagues—near and far—all of whom are dealing with Covid-19 across their geopolitical locations on the globe. In the very early days of the pandemic, my global team of consultants (Charlés, 2019) called me from their homes in Kosovo, Syria, Guatemala, and San Antonio, Texas, to see how I was doing.

I live in one of the communities in Massachusetts that, today, has the highest rate of transmission of Covid-19. Telling you of this notable fact, I am reminded of how we used to talk about the village communities across Guinea during Ebola—some villages had it much worse than others, and we couldn't always figure out why. We had multiple maps spread throughout the situation rooms, in which we tracked areas of high transmission and new unexpected outbreaks. Knowing this data was critical to our response. This was how we, the mental health team, focused our efforts of psychosocial support and mhGAP training. Now, in Massachusetts, I am living in one of these areas.

The week of the March 11 declaration by WHO of Covid-19 as a pandemic, I was in the midst of a slew of emails and Skype meetings with colleagues across Southeast Asia and Europe. I was invited to deliver a training in family therapy, as part of a multilateral project within an international organization. I had agreed to the TOR, had my plane ticket in hand, and was ready to depart on March 20 to a city on the other side of the globe. I was excited—I'd be going to a country I had not been to for over a decade and would be located in a region that was also a keen research interest of mine. Pre-pandemic, our team in the Skype calls had discussed the kind of gear we would need to do such a training. We expected disruption because of the virus. In our calls, we brainstormed the kinds of situation we were likely to face, quite aware of the ongoing fluidity across the globe.

This is part of what a multilateral project looks like, for me: It is systemic by nature, fluid and dynamic, all the time, every time. It is also, of course, defined by coordinated partnerships between countries, that is, states and state actors. That brings its own complexity. Thus, our planning did not stop until one country after another began its own version of containment by closing down its borders. The training was postponed, then cancelled. It was another few days, or maybe a week, before the magnitude of the pandemic hit my own community, when shoppers began to hoard products, and fear and anxiety seemed to be the order of the day.

Multilateral Coordination and Multilateral Complexity: Where Is the Front Line?

Today, three months into my life during Covid-19, things are not exactly calmer, but they are more routinized than they were a few months ago. In Massachusetts, my living and my working mutually shape the other in a constant way that I cannot turn off, as I felt that I did in Guinea each day when I returned to my hotel by the 6 p.m. curfew.

Each week in Guinea, I traveled to a different village for training—and on those days, I was working and living EVD 24/7. But I was almost always "home" by the weekend, when I could do absolutely nothing except go to the pool, watch TV5, or read and text my friends. In 2015 Guinea, Ebola seemed to be some kind of bizarre anomaly that my friends in Trinidad and Tobago, Sri Lanka, or San Antonio did not have to deal with up front, nor fully grasp. In those three months in Guinea, I messaged them all the time; hearing about their worlds helped give me an escape from mine. Today, in Covid-19, we are all in the up front, together. I am still texting these dear ones now during Covid-19, but of course, there is no escape to be had.

We are all here at the ultramarathon, running and/or walking, each at our own pace, sometimes disoriented and sometimes mobilized, comparing notes as we go, and helping each other along as we all try to get to the next mile. In both emergencies, I have found the use of ICTs incredibly critical. "When the fabric of social support is ripped by isolation, it should be patched as soon as possible with available technological means, including phones, tablets, and social media" (Huremovic, 2019, pp 104–5).

The kind of work that I do as a public mental health professional means that I am very much in a "front line" state of mind in a public health emergency. Whether it is quarantine, shelter-in-place, or social distancing, the psychological and emotional effects of living inside a pandemic are profound.

> From a psychological perspective, the consequences of social distancing are summed up in two words—isolation and uncertainty. All measures of social distancing result in various degrees of isolation. Isolation in social distancing can be quite palpable, physical (contact barriers, protective equipment, physical separation by glass or locked doors) and symbolic (separation from loved ones, inability to read facial expressions from masked faces, feel a human touch on one's skin, inability to make out a human shape underneath protective equipment).
>
> (Huremović, 2019, p. 91)

Talking about my work in the EVD 2014 epidemic before Covid-19 seemed to be some kind of rarefied conversation. It was prestigious for me when I mentioned the work in professional talks, but also, it was quite niche in its specialization. It didn't seem to apply much to my audiences' everyday life. That seems to me to have changed completely.

I have found, ironically, that my time in Guinea has helped me develop a robust capacity to support mental health workers during Covid-19. I did not realize that my EVD response experience would be so valuable in this particular way. Yet it is so very relevant right now. For instance, I deliver telemental health services to clients as part of a health network, and so witness every day a spectrum of effects from the pandemic on my clients' lives. They all have different reactions to the pandemic, and each of them is affected in very different ways. I understand some of these reactions in ways my clients do not always realize.

"Building Back Better": What I Learned from EVD 2014 (That I Bring to Covid-19)

Although I had prepared for my deployment to Conakry by taking numerous modules organized through the WHO learning platform, including many on Infection Prevention and Control, it wasn't until I arrived that I realized the implications of Ebola on people's physical and social contact with each other. During the outbreak, it was unsafe for people to touch each other. I myself stopped wearing rings on my fingers; it was too risky as I didn't always have water to wash my hands and had to rely on hand sanitizer often in Guinea. No rings mitigated my risk; it was a simple, easy thing to change. And it stuck. It took two more years before I put my rings back on, so changed was my view on handwashing after Ebola.

The risks of transmission due to physical contact meant a drastic change in norms that had a profound effect on people's everyday life in Guinea, including but certainly not limited to the rituals around death and dying. During EVD, affected family members could not physically express emotions with their loved ones, neither alive nor deceased and in preparation for burial. This was a key issue for our MHPSS team; family members' reticence could often be tied to fear and worry about their loved one's illness and possible or eventual death. Many deaths were kept secret. At the time I arrived in Guinea, enough of those deaths had occurred that it was already law that only the state could bury the deceased. In turn, those Guinéens who worked for the state to conduct those burials were shunned, stigmatized, and ostracized.

My community, just like everyone else's in Massachusetts, and everywhere, is itself in the midst of rapid change as it adjusts and introduces new norms as part of preparedness and response to Covid-19. For us, at the early stages of pandemic response, infection prevention and control are a critical thing to norm, and to norm correctly and safely. Norms are collective by nature. However, they must be implemented individually, repeatedly, across an extended period of time and circumstance to be effective.

In Guinea, we experienced routine, repeated, graphic issues of what we termed reticence in communities, some including ongoing violence, either about the nature of EVD 2014, its origins, or its response. In one town in Guinea during my mission, WHO staff were threatened and forced to evacuate. This fear or reluctance had its basis in mistrust of the government and weakened state-citizen relations, pre-dating EVD 2014, but further exacerbated by it. My consultant work in Guinea took place against this backdrop. My life in the U.S. right now feels somewhat parallel to it.

In my world in the U.S. today, there is ongoing *reticence*, as we would call it in Guinea, about the changing norms. There is fear and deep angst about what it means to live with the potential harmful implications of your physical contact with another person, whether a loved one or an acquaintance. There is grief and sadness about how to bury and mourn the death of loved ones during a health emergency in which physical contact can have deadly implications. There is frustration, fear, and loss of livelihood. GDPs across the globe are contracting right and left. My clients and my students reference for me the newness and the pain of these changing norms in the places they live and work. I can feel them, too. But they are not new for me.

I think there is a pain in that early development of these norms that I did not witness in Guinea, because my arrival was eighteen months into their establishment. I learned very quickly from watching everyone else's behavior. I learned in theory how to mitigate risk of EVD transmission, and then I learned in an embodied way once in Guinea what that meant with regard to relational interactions. I had many hundreds of consultant colleagues to model from, in vivo, as they enacted the norms in front of me in real time. That particular learning was very efficient; it was easy to acclimate to existing norms. Here in Massachusetts, I am at the start of the marathon of new norms, of preparedness, response, and "Building Back Better."

PFA and mhGAP: Useful Beyond Measure, Relevant Beyond Emergency

Dear Shoufi Mafi,

One last question, but first—a story. The first week I arrived, I traveled with my team to work in Dubreka, where we did a "PFA" training for 100 community health workers. Most of our time is spent giving trainings like this. In addition to the trainings, there is an overall goal for us as a team: as much as we can, to focus on the support of the ministry of health and mental health to build their health system so they in turn can support the mental health needs of the population re: Ebola and post Ebola. This is fascinating work but it is really so difficult. I work closely with one of the ministers who has been working on the issue for years. Now, there is an opportunity to build back better in this crisis. But it is not easy. How do you convince an entire government to give money where they never gave it before? How do you help your host country national team to do that?

In Guinea, although most of my colleagues seemed to see me on the "front line" of the Ebola response, I do not remember that I ever felt it in that way. It was not me that had to do any convincing of a foreign government; I did not conduct every day the trainings in PFA or mhGAP. I was not the one meeting with the family directly affected by EVD. As a foreigner, an international consultant working inside Guinea as a guest, I supported the host country national team, who I knew would be in Guinea long after I was gone. They are more than able to do their work; however, during an epidemic, or a pandemic—any emergency—we have extra opportunities to "Build Back Better." So that is what we focused on trying to do.

Seeing the Start of the Race, and Also
Far Beyond It

In Guinea as part of the EVD 2014 response team, I did all kinds of things, including training at times, supervising training all the time, creating training modules, meeting consistently with my team as well as with other MHPSS teams, state officials, and international/country partners, all the while listening very closely to what happens to families in the context of EVD. Yes, I lived in Guinea, I was inside the outbreak, and I learned everything I needed to know about Covid-19 during EVD 2014, but I still would not say I was on the front lines. I worked directly with people on the front lines, but I was only living in the proximity as a result of the deployment to Guinea.

Today, however, I feel very much on the front lines, although I have not been deployed anywhere. The frontline came to me. Now, we all have had the experience of deployment. Fortunately, I'm here with a set of double description lenses, thanks to Guinea. They help me see the start of the race, and also, far beyond it.

Note

1 The International Health Regulations is a regulatory instrument that is binding on members of the UN 196 states. The IHR creates both rights and obligations for member states, one of which is that every party to it is required to develop national core capacity to detect and respond effectively to a public health emergency.

References

Charlés, L. (July 2015a). Long live Shoufi Mafi! Family therapy in the age of global mental health. Family Therapy Magazine, 14 (4), 34–39.

Charlés, L. (October 14, 2015b). *Supporting mental health and psychosocial support (MHPSS) in the context of the Ebola outbreak in West Africa.* OLLU Faculty Development Workshop, San Antonio, TX.

Charlés, L. (2019). My global team of family therapy consultants: Seven commandments of my method. In Charlés, L. & Nelson, T. (Eds.), Family therapy supervision in extraordinary settings: Illustrations of systemic approaches in everyday clinical work. London: Routledge.

Faregh, N. & Charlés, L. (April 28, 2017). Re-thinking the role of family and culture in the aftermath of epidemics. In V. di Nicola (Moderator), *Paper Session 4: Power and Family Dynamics.* The Society for the Study of Psychiatry and Culture (SSPC) Annual Conference, Philadelphia, PA.

Faregh, N., Tounkara, A. and Soumaoro, K. (2019). The Role of family and culture in extreme adversity: Psychosocial response to the Ebola Virus Disease (EVD) Epidemic in Guinea, West Africa. In Charlés, L. & Samarasinghe, G. (Eds.). *Family systems & global humanitarian mental health: Approaches in the field.* New York: Springer.

Huremović, D. (2019). *Psychiatry of pandemics: A mental health response to infection outbreak.* New York: Springer.

Longuépée, J. (June 17, 2015). Guinée: a la poursuite d' "Ebola Zéro". *Le Figaro*, Mercredi.

Pearson, H. (June 24, 2015). Building back better from West Africa's Ebola outbreak. Mental Health Innovation Network. Retrieved from www.mhinnovation.net/blog/2015/jun/24/building-back-better-west-africa%E2%80%99s-ebola-outbreak

St. Victor, G. and Ahmed, S. (2019). The Importance of Culture in Managing Mental Health Response to Pandemics (pp. 55-64). In Huremović, D. (Ed). Psychiatry of pandemics: A mental health response to infection outbreak. New York: Springer.

The Office of Governor Charlie Baker and Lt. Governor Karyn Polito (2020). *Baker-Polito administration announces COVID-19 community tracing collaborative to further mitigate the spread of virus* [Press release]. Retrieved from www.mass.gov/news/baker-polito-administration-announces-Covid-19-community-tracing-collaborative-to-further

Wallace-Wells, B. (June 12, 2020). Can Coronavirus contact tracing survive reopening? The New Yorker, June 8 & 15, 2020.

World Health Organization (2008). *Mental Health Gap Action Programme: Scaling up care for mental, nuerological and substance use disorders.* Geneva: World Health Organization. https://apps.who.int/iris/handle/10665/43809

11

FAMILY THERAPY TRAINING IN A MULTILATERAL PROJECT

The Transformative Process of a 3D Role-Play in Beirut

In 2013 and 2014, I went to Libya to deliver a set of family therapy training modules. The modules were designed for public mental health professionals working with ex-combatants from the Feb 17 Revolution, which had ended the 40 year Qadaffi regime. Shortly after that experience ended, I began to work with the World Health Organization (WHO) on a set of projects focused in Syria. In every project, role-plays have played a critical part. In this chapter, I want to share with you a role-play that took place in a training for Syrian public mental health workers in Beirut. First, however, I need to take you to visit some other role plays, in a few other places. We'll start in San Antonio, Texas, then head to Manila, in the Philippines, before bringing it all back home to Lebanon and Syria.

I remember quite vividly my first role-play. I was a family therapy master's student in Dr. Glen Gardner's Introduction to Family Therapy class, in San Antonio, Texas. Dr. Gardner pulled a desk into the center of the room.

These were the very old-fashioned school desks, large objects fit more for teaching 9–year olds than a class of graduate students. No matter; the 20 or so of us in the room quickly made a circle around Dr. Gardner, eager to get as close as possible, enthralled and excited to hear and see what we could, and to learn about this thing called 'family therapy.'

Although I retained nothing of what was actually *said* in the exercise, I still remember how it *felt*—the anticipation of it, the aliveness. Through this very simple gesture, Dr. Gardner had made another world accessible to us. The theoretical basis of what I was learning became, in an instant, *real*. Dr. Gardner brought to us the intense, transformative complexity of what family therapy can be like to perform, and to learn. He had made an entirely other world visible to us.

That first role play took place 25 years ago. In between that time and today, as a professor and trainer, I have been part of countless family therapy role-plays—and I am not alone. Today, progressive family therapy training incorporates role-play of all kinds, live demonstrations, and the use of simulation to bring the multiple dimensions of family therapy "in the room" experience to trainees in real time. However progressive it may be, essentially, the basic idea is the same as it was in Dr. Gardner's class. How do we replicate the family system in a training context, in a way that best enhances the learning of trainees?

Family Therapy Role-Plays with the Manileños

In Manila, in 2002, I had a large class of students, much too large I thought, for my typical role-play activities. There wasn't enough time to engage everyone, and I was panicking. I was teaching in a large auditorium, with stadium seats, angled upwards, while I was down at the bottom, on the stage, level with the first row. I asked a group of students to formulate a scenario for a "typical case" in their work, and to step briefly outside the classroom to do so. I did not ask to be informed of it ahead of time. This was just a hunch—I wanted to keep the same process I faced in real life. To my surprise, that worked so well I've kept it constant in my work. But back then, I only did it because I didn't have time to listen to them, as I had about 30 other students left in the classroom. How could I involve them? Thirty observers would not work in Manila. What else could I do? (Charlés, 2007).

I asked for one third of the students to come down to the front of the room, and stand alongside me. I told them that they would each have two minutes to sit in the chair as the "therapist in the room." I would keep time, and after two minutes, I'd tap their shoulder to stop. These days I ask someone in the class to time it, so I don't have to. This allows me a bit more freedom to write down the trainee's questions, which has been important in the feedback portion of the exercise.

Next, after the trainee finishes their two minutes, the following person in the line will sit down in the chair to continue the interview with the family, who will behave as if it is the same clinician—no need to repeat anything or do introductions each time. This process continues until all that first third of the trainees have had a turn in the chair, which will take about 20 minutes. The role-play family is instructed to continue in their role as if they have the same therapist; the folks in the therapy chair, meanwhile, are asked to continue as if it is one interview, not a series of ten brief ones.

The round-robin approach I ended up using my first time in Manila accomplishes several tasks at the same time. First, it helps students focus on a line of therapy inquiry (as if they are on a team, already, behind the mirror) with some intention and readiness. Second, it focuses their attention in a helpful, organized way that is both participant and observer. Third, it makes them think about each other differently—as a collective brain of clinicians, a team.

I do then a robust reflection at the end of the exercise, perhaps also 20 minutes. By robust, I mean that everyone who wants to say something should be given a chance to speak, at least until saturation is reached. When I do the reflecting/discussion, I have learned it's best to do it from "inside the experience" to "outside." That is, the "family" is asked their reflections first, then the "therapists," then the "observers." I focus on the Singer (2005) questions: Did they feel heard, understood, respected and accepted? What questions helped that? What hindered it? What was it like to be in the chair as a family member? As a clinician? An observer?

When it comes to talking to the "clinicians," I always try to speak about the questions that worked well, what each person did well, as a way to encourage this type of exercise in an ongoing way. I don't want the students to be discouraged. I make my feedback direct, immediate, and based on the "data"—the words the trainee actually used. I take copious notes, almost as if I am transcribing the trainees' questions and comments. I have all sorts of questions for them about their process. What was it like when they sat down? Stood up? What was going through their mind when they asked a question? What had they noticed happening before they sat down?

Inevitably, new trainees will say two minutes went by much too slowly. Advanced trainees say it was not enough time. Many trainees will pick up on something said earlier by a classmate, and continue it as a line of questioning; others may pick up on who in the family is not being talked to, or what is not being asked, and start an entirely new line of questioning. Sometimes, if I need to focus the observers of the role-play in a more directive fashion, I have them focus their attention on just one "family member," and their client experience in the role-play session. In the feedback, they can speak from this particular view, sometimes providing descriptions otherwise unattainable. Virtually everything that happens in a role-play like this is useful for training.

I have gradually increased the complexity of this basic, essential role-play exercise as my training work became more complex, and occurred inside humanitarian, complex emergencies and in multi-lingual formats. In most trainings I do outside the U.S., where I am conducting a multi-day training in family therapy, I will do at least three role-plays a day. Most of these trainings are at least five days in length, although sometimes they may be as many as 12 days. By the end of the training, sometimes trainees have lost count how many role-plays they have done, and I always think that is a good thing.

The role-plays that have come after Manila are not all exactly like the one I did that first time on the stage. However, that example remains a fundamental, practical, constant, innovative, developing *in situ* type of training format I use. In other words, San Antonio opened the door, and Manila became the foundation that built the house.

WHO Psychotherapeutic Interventions Course in Libya: An Invitation to Curiosity

In Libya, the objectives of my technical training for the WHO were to introduce and scale up participants' skill set in basics of family therapy interviewing and practice. Specifically, the training delivery focused on enhancing participants' use of family therapy methods to work with ex-combatants in post-conflict Libya. However, skills and methods I addressed in the training were intended to be relevant to any family's presenting problem within the current socio-cultural context of Libya and the participants' respective work locations. This latter intention was addressed in role-plays and case scenarios brought by the trainees from their direct personal and professional experience.

At the time of the training for WHO, family therapy was a new practice in the Libyan context. Thus, this training focused on essential and introductory aspects of engaging and working face-to-face with families and with family configurations in the post-conflict psychosocial context. The training content was put into practice through multiple daily role-play exercises (sometimes two or three per day), small group and large group demonstrations, and experiential exercises. Theoretical content and didactic lecture was used only to introduce knowledge that served the actual practice of family therapy within the context of ex-combatants' psychosocial needs in Libya. The participation of the trainees' and their willingness to engage with me and the other trainees was critical to the outcome.

Sometimes, I do an experiential activity before a role-play, so I can get a sense of how expressive a group might be, or to learn what is interesting, new, or familiar for them. In Libya, I was truly starting from scratch. Geographical proximity was no help at all. Although I had lived in Cairo for a year, right next door to Libya, only a few years earlier, that turned out to be no indication for me of familiarity. Libya has a completely different history than Egypt, in so many ways, despite being its geographic neighbor. Further, after the end of the Qadaffi regime, the society was opening up for the first time. Unless you were a Libyan who had lived in Libya, there was so much you didn't know about its tribes and clans.

We began with introductions in which participants had to do an icebreaker: "Something no one here knows about me," then continued by performing a qualitative exercise to demonstrate the idea of "entering cultures" (Green, 1996, personal communication), which focused on interviewing from an ethnographic understanding of another's experience. Trainees were asked to focus on the line of inquiry questions observed and judge how well or not the questions allowed for dialogue.

This group discussion was a way for me to assess how observant the group was, and how willing they were to engage in specific questioning topics or challenge my own ideas. They were very curious about the entire process, which I thought was a very good sign. The next day when we began family therapy role-plays they were incredibly engaged and interactive, although perhaps somewhat nervous.

The first role-plays focused on introducing one's self to a family, explaining roles and responsibilities of their psychosocial work, and opening questions in a family therapy interview. In role-plays, any trainee who was not interacting as a therapist or a family member was instructed to observe and write down all the questions asked in the role play. Feedback on these first two days included comments such as: "It was helpful to learn how to share in a group"; "Flexibility is an important aspect when dealing with different families"; "Gaining the family's trust must be done by establishing rapport"; "Focus on clinical interaction is interesting for us as we are used to focusing only on theory"; "Time management is hard for us but very important and you got us to do it." The trainees had only 20 minutes to do each role-play in the training.

In role-plays, we focused on practicing: Questioning; Attending to verbal and non-verbal expression; Joining with each family member; Modifying body posture to reflect interest and respect; Dealing with complex family interaction and conflict; Managing personal curiosity v. therapeutic curiosity (Flemons, 1996). The material content provided by the trainees in the role-plays included Families with an ex-combatant experiencing sadness, fearfulness, withdrawal; families with a loss of status or resources as a result of the conflict; ex-combatants dealing with survival guilt and loss of friends; ex-combatants dealing with loss of limbs and status as able-bodied persons; role of daughters/women during the revolution; and what it means to be a "rebel" post-revolution.

Family role-play scenarios in Libya during my time there nearly always included at least three generations, including extended family living in or outside the home. I was told this was very typical of Libyan families, and thus was glad to see it reflected in the group role-plays. Small group role-plays consisted of six to eight people. In order to keep the content relevant to the contemporary context in post-conflict Libya, role-play scenarios were always created by trainees in their small groups.

3D Shelter: Family Therapy Training in Syria

Family systems training is ripe with role-play scenarios; however, scenarios must be as realistic as possible, reflecting the nature of the families' lives. In Syria, in 2016, families living in shelters across the country were no longer an exception to the norm; it was the norm. Forced displacement of families in a country in the midst of years of armed conflict can take on many forms. Shelter is sometimes concrete, sometimes metaphor. In Syria, shelters differ across governorates in a number of ways, with regard to who is the organizing/funding partner, the types of spaces families use in a shelter, or perhaps other reasons. How could we, in a training, help to bring in data from the country's situation (Charlés, 2015)? How could we simulate families in shelters in Syria inside the training room?

While there can be many differences across family shelters in the country during that time in the still ongoing Syrian war, there were a few commonalities worth noting:

(1) Living in a shelter means an extreme lack of privacy for behaviors that are normally private or perhaps, hidden.
(2) Quantity of family members changes dramatically, with a lack of walls that would normally divide a house into rooms, or a neighborhood into houses.
(3) Families living together in family units in the shelter are not necessarily blood kin. Even if they are, they may not have ever lived together before nor had much contact with each other, before the war. Thus, it can be become a new family system.
(4) Everyone living in the shelter, including the people in charge of its operation on the ground, are also affected by the conditions in the war. No one is immune. Thus, the shelter can become a microcosm of the larger system in the war.

One of my colleagues in the training, a particularly artistic and expressive clinician and supervisor in Syria, suggested that in order to maximize the utility of system concepts in this group of MHPSS professionals in a family systems training, a typical "role-play" can easily become a multiple scenario "play," or "performance." This performance could perhaps allow a way for trainees to experience, learn about, and discuss their own clinical skills and challenges. The activity would be built on role-plays, but drastically increasing the system of actors inside of it. It could reflect the nature of what the system looked like inside the country at the time, and poignantly, the many MHPSS challenges the families were facing on a daily basis.

We gave the following instructions to the trainees, after considering them and reflecting on them the night before.

(1) Begin: In your group, choose one person as observer. All others should choose a role of a person/family in a shelter. Make sure everyone has a role to play in the scenario. Together, choose the scenario of a family system that is likely occuring inside this shelter, or is similar to what you have learned from your clients takes place in the shelter. Take a full 20 minutes to discuss this so your performance is as rich and detailed as it can be. Then, if possible, go up to your hotel room or wherever you have access to some of your belongings. Choose items from your things that you can use as props for the scenario of the family in the shelter.

(2) Observer Role: The observer should act as a person who is unseen, unnoticed, and strictly in the role of observer in the scenario. The observer should not be privy to the scenario planning; they should not be present for the preparation discussion. As observer of the family-in-the-shelter system, take detailed notes on what you see, and what you hear. Keep interpretations in a separate column in your notes and focus on using your sensory input: what you see, hear, smell, touch. Focus especially on the dialogue, conversation, behaviors—in other words, verbal and non-verbal behavior. Observe inside the system, walk around, explore what is happening inside the shelter scenario. Do this the entire time of the performance.

(3) Role-Play Performance: All performances should occur at the same time, simultaneously, in different parts of the room. Choose a place for your shelter and remain there. The point of the exercise is for the participants to fully experience the context of their own shelter scenario. Trainers will walk around to observe across the scenarios, but remain silent. Trainers can speak to or comment on overall themes at the end of the performances and exercise.

(4) Discussion: An experienced trainer should coordinate the discussion by participants after the activity. Each observer should be brought to the front of the room to share his/her observations and experiences. After an observer from each group has spoken, the trainers should offer their own observations.

(5) Post-Role-Play: Roles performed within the scenario, i.e. "the things that cannot be discussed but are seen" should be incorporated and utilized in other parts of the training.

We had suspected this exercise would be fruitful. However, I think we were all very surprised at the extent of its richness and sensitivity. The room became a loud, noisy place, full of action. Hotel staff came down to see what was happening; our NGO partner brought in a cameraman (they had been filming a short segment in another part of the hotel for the project, which was funded by the EU) and, with permission from the training cohort, he filmed some of the sequences we were witnessing.

Our training took place in a basement of a four-star hotel in Beirut. Normally, such a cavernous room would be a bit too formal and cold for a family therapy training. However, for this exercise it was perfect. The large, enclosed space, away from the people traffic of the hotel, made it amenable for the exercise in a way we had not anticipated.

So, what did we witness? I remember seeing the absence of privacy. I remember seeing people sleeping in cramped areas, their clothes hanging everywhere. In one corner of the room, I saw a young woman alone, and a man who was following her around and bothering her, as if stalking her, illustrating for me the high risk of SGBV in shelters. I had heard this discussed in numerous cases and clinical examples, the risk of SGBV in war and in particular, in this war. But, seeing even a hint of it simulated in a role-play was profound. I felt the secret—what my colleague had referred to—those things that could not be said, could not be seen, right there in the room.

In another corner, all the men were sitting in one part of their shelter, faux-smoking and drinking. Next to them, several female trainee participants had crayoned moustaches on pieces of masking tape, placed the tape under their noses, and were joining in the men's conversation with gusto. At the same time, in the other, quieter parts of that same group's shelter, women were caring for children. It was such a powerful contrast. Then, the lights all went out in the room! Someone had turned out the lights in the ballroom. The lights going off was a way to remind us how electricity was not a given in the shelters or in the country at that time, a condition applicable to all scenarios in the room.

In another corner, I could see how several of the trainees had brought some of their luggage down to the basement, to make small makeshift tables, using scarves to hide small sleeping places, simulating walls that also did not exist in the shelters. In the front of the room, it looked as if a young girl was about to married off; there was loud, happy singing and dancing, chanting and ululations. Such a difference from the first scene. One of my colleagues remembers seeing a scenario of families in line for foodbaskets at the shelter. In that line, she remembers seeing a man trying to molest a young girl in the line.

Someone brought me into the dancing, breaking the fourth wall rule and simultaneously, allowing for other trainees to grab their smart phones take photos of the trainer dancing to Syrian music. Everything that I witnessed seemed somewhat exaggerated (as often happens in a family therapy role-play), but also, full of profound kernels of truth.

The Beirut role-play exercise was one of the most incredible experiences I have had in my work. As I wrote in my report to the NGO who had brought me on as a consultant, it is important to point out how very unplanned it was, how organic. It was a powerful moment to safely show, not just tell, the conditions that pervade family life during the war. Further, the exercise was incredibly useful to help our discussion of systems theory and systems exploration, and thus, more precise treatment planning and family assessment. Like a living, breathing simulation of a genogram (or, perhaps, a sophisticated, animated, and intense performance version of Virginia Satir's sculpting), our work as trainers was enriched by the participants' expressions of family life during the Syrian war.

The psychiatrist Dr. Richard Mollica, of the Harvard Program in Refugee Trauma, has talked about the importance of observing not only traumatic incident effects on families, but the full range of human experience that accompanies adaptation to forced displacement or other traumatic events (Mollica, 2006). Here we had a living, breathing example of that performed before our very eyes. As the exercise went on, the performances became more dramatic in the visual and verbal expression, such that we all felt as if we were no longer in a training room—we were in another dimension of current family life in Syria. It was as if the trainees had brought the war inside the room.

Significantly, the origins of the idea that helped formulate this exercise came directly from the Syrian participants in the training, and our relationship that had developed over time. I had worked so hard over the years to do the thing Singer (2005) had discussed—to help them feel heard, understood, respected and accepted—as I supported their supervision work during the WHO projects. Nevertheless, this exercise was not something I could have thought of on my own, no matter how many years nor countries in which I've been identified as a Subject Matter Expert.

In fact, it was during our debriefings each day that we, as co-trainers, had conceived the idea in a hotel room, as a team. Then, as in all relational systemic work, it took on a life of its own between us as co-trainers, which was enhanced yet further in the hands of the trainees that day. The 3D Shelter was the name we called this exercise. It was a role-play, yes. But it was also so very many other things, a three dimensional, intense portrait of family life during the Syrian war in 2016. It took about 90 minutes. Yet, looking back, I think perhaps it had been in the making for years.

References

Charlés, L. (2007). Cultural competency as a relational process: Scenes from a Family Therapy context in the Philippines. *Qualitative Inquiry, 13* (8), 1160–1176.

Charlés, L. L. (2015). Scaling up family therapy in fragile, conflict-affected states. *Family Process, 54* (3), 545–558.

Flemons, D. (1996). *Of one mind: The logic of hypnosis, the practice of therapy.* New York: W. W. Néorton.

Mollica, R. F. (2006). *Healing invisible wounds: Paths to hope and recovery in a violent world.* New York: Harcourt.

Singer, M. (2005). A twice-told tale: A phenomenological inquiry into clients' perceptions of therapy. *Journal of Marital and Family Therapy, 31,* 269–281

Strauss, A., & Corbin, J. (2008). *Basics of qualitative research: Techniques and procedures for developing grounded theory (3rd ed.).* Thousand Oaks, CA: Sage.

PART III

DEBRIEF AND REINTEGRATION

12

LEAVING HOME
Desk Work and Preparation

I've checked in to my flight to Asia, which, from Boston, is, of course, a long-haul flight. At one time, I thought the six–hour trek to Paris from Boston was long. Today, that six- hour trip feels quite brief. The 22+ hour flights to Asia usually start with a thirteen–hour leg, then after a transfer in someplace like Doha or Dubai, another six-hour leg to my final destination. This is my first trip to Bangkok. But I've flown quite a lot to South Asia. I am accustomed to and prepared for the long-haul flight, and yes, it's exhausting! But it's part of the preparation, it's part of the work, to manage that exhaustion in a productive way. I need to arrive ready to work. So, there are many other things to think about besides the flight. But the flight is where it usually begins.

I'm hardly the first person to have had such a steady stream of work-related travel in my life. But I've learned a few things over the years and I am always looking for new, useful tips. Whatever the class of flight (in case you were wondering, my flights are always paid for, but also, always in Economy class. If I have the right kind of frequent flyer miles, I may be able to upgrade one leg or another), it is a very long time to be in such a small space with hundreds of people. Since the outbound trip involves a first leg that is a solid 12 hours, I can sleep. In the brief transfer, I'll use my miles again to do a trip to the lounge, where I can eat breakfast, maybe freshen up with a shower or change of clothes, and most importantly, drink loads of water. I need sleep, but usually, I need water more.

The next leg is quicker than the first. But because it is yet another night time flight I am at so much more risk of being disoriented. In the second flight, I will eat (again), maybe take some coffee or sip prosecco— depending on my mood—and, always, I drink lots and lots of water. I eat a little bit even if I am not hungry, because I usually have no idea when I'll eat again. (On another note, I usually travel with a type of nutrition bar, one for each day I'm gone; they are easy to pack and keep well. They are better for energy though, than meals, I've found. Sometimes, I've had to eat them as a meal—one time, three days straight—but that is another story).

After eating, once I've relaxed into my seat on the plane, there is nothing else I attempt to do. I do not read. I do not prepare for the upcoming training. I do not send emails to colleagues. I stop everything, and I sleep. Sleep is critical. Sleep is very healing at this point. Also: water.

When I eventually arrive, in Colombo, or Tashkent, or Bangkok, I will sleep again. I'll check into my room at the hotel, and I'll sleep for about four to six hours before I begin to have meetings. If I am in Asia, typically, I will arrive at 6 or 8 in the morning. Sometimes I can check in early at the hotel, sometimes, I cannot. I try to prepare for both possibilities.

I've never been to Bangkok, and my experience when I arrive in a new city on the other side of the globe is that I can easily find a way to keep myself awake if I need to. Occasionally, in spite of the demands to my changing circadian rhythm, I find I come fully alive at such moments. Perhaps I can check my bags with the hotel and walk around for a few hours? Maybe I can order a pot of tea and sit in the lobby, writing? Strolling in a new city, to me, after flying 24 hours is much easier after a shower and a lovely block of sleep, but if necessary, I can do it without that. Eventually, I'll get my shower; I'll get my sleep. The promise of sleep in itself is enough; it is a great reassurance for me. It becomes an incentive very quickly, sleep. That, and water.

A while back, I read a lovely piece in the *Journal of Systemic Therapy* by Michael Ungar (2003), about the importance of travel for the family therapist. Early in my career, I gravitated toward pieces like this. Elsewhere, I have told the story of how I met Fred Piercy (Charlés & Piercy, 2003); our first contact started because of the piece he had written on being a family therapist trainer in Indonesia, also in JST (Piercy, 1998). I have since met Michael Ungar (the FT world is a small one), and have also become friendly colleagues with Fred. Most of my colleagues these days travel all the time, to do workshops, to go to conferences, to be a guest or visiting instructor somewhere outside their home country. Everyone is always going somewhere.

Travel and both its monotonous and adventurous details are commonly the things I am asked about by colleagues, trainees in the U.S., and conference participants who want to hear about what I do. Travel is something we all can relate to. I don't think it's particularly unique for anyone who travels a great deal, but it is certainly interesting to compare notes and borrow tips from other folks who travel so much more than I do. When I am working multilaterally, in a project with many people, with three or more countries engaged, I am bound to learn a ton of things. There are always people who have traveled to twice as many countries as me, who are incredibly savvy, and full of stories.

At home, in the U.S., people are often amazed at where I've been, or where I'm going, or what I've seen. For instance, before I went to Libya for the first time, part of my family and I went to a destination wedding in Jamaica. At the resort, by the pool, a family member seemed so shocked I was going to Libya, and also, wondered why I didn't seem to be afraid to go? This puzzled her. I trusted my colleague who had invited me, and I knew or felt I knew, how to mitigate my risk. But some things, and places, are hard to explain. The world is so big and so small, all at the same time.

In the last training I did, at the time of this writing it was the Maldives, I worked with several consultants who were something like "rock stars" to me. They travel as much as rock stars, which is why I call them that. They are not family therapists, by the way. They are usually trained in other health and mental health professions. They might be nurses, psychiatrists, maybe psychologists, or social workers. My rock star co-trainers have a slightly different professional tilt to viewing the experience in the training room than I do, but I often find we have a great deal in common. Their stories are both hilarious and familiar, and feel like home to me.

My colleagues' stories in Bangkok were also so very unbelievable! (Hearing their stories, I had a good taste of what it is like for people at home to hear my own). For every story one of my new colleagues told me, I had to pinch myself to make sure I was not dreaming. For every unbelievable story I told, they matched me with another, wilder one. This was delightful to experience. A colleague based in London looked over at me at one point on a deployment, smiled, winked, then said: "We need to sit down and compare notes!" Yes! We do.

Here are the questions I am routinely asked about my multilateral work as a family therapist:

"What do you do to prepare to work in different countries?"

"Do you get paid for this work?"

"Aren't you afraid?"

"What does your partner/spouse/family think? Don't you miss them? Don't they worry?"

"All those countries you've been to, and you've never seen the movie *Aladdin*?" (Just the other day one of my students asked me this).

Saturday night, 48 hours from writing this, I will have dinner with two colleagues, my international co-trainers in the project in Bangkok. I met with them this week virtually, one is in the UK and the other in Europe, to begin our discussions about the training we are doing together. The European colleague, a psychiatrist I met last year in a training we did in Uzbekistan, is super cool. After we finish in Bangkok, in about seven days, the UK colleague, who I've never worked with before, and I will fly to the Maldives. There, we'll do another version of the Bangkok training, with a different group of participants from four countries in South Asia and two countries in Africa.

In addition to my family therapy expertise, which is something that I am bringing to the table, there is always so much more to learn, starting with the complexity of working with two other experts, seasoned "rock stars", not family therapy experts but expert trainers all the same. Between us, we represent three+ countries, a half dozen languages, and plenty of experiences that could easily enhance (but just as easily further complicate) our mission.

Each of us has had different working experiences with the UN office that is bringing us, and also, with the country that we are working in. So that is a plus, in a way. It could be a problem, too. Actually—we don't know, not yet. Everything is infused with meaning; yet, at the same time, not every meaning is relevant to the mission. These missions are time limited and at an intense pace that allows for very little reflection until it is over. Still, one becomes dynamic with the process, *in situ*. Doing this work, I find I am living in a state that is fluid and dynamic all the time, every single time. I do my best to hold on to that complexity. For me, preparing myself and other family therapists for this is preparing them for a macro perspective that is similar to what they see in work with family systems, but instead, is focused on states and the international system.

One key aspect of all of the multilateral projects I have done is the notion of "desk work." Spelled out in every single contract I have had, it essentially refers to the one, two, or few days that you are paid to do preparation work or completion work from home as part of the upcoming project. Some projects have more desk work than others; some projects are *all* desk work.

In family therapy, we have usually a "pre-session" or briefing, to prepare for the case or session; maybe also we have a post session. I often feel that desk work is the parallel of a family therapy pre-session —the beginning or the key part of your process. In multilateral work, it's also you being paid for your preparation time, your work that is not necessarily taking place "in the field." So, like a pre-session, desk work must be used well, in a theoretically sound and also practical way.

Desk work is me, and me alone. Although sometimes I am sent concept papers, briefing notes, or background, no one tells me what to do when I am paid for desk work; there isn't a supervisor to organize or administer to me. That is also desk work: It's self-directed; you have to be sharp enough to prepare by knowing what you don't know. Knowing what you don't know is a kind of expertise, too.

Also, desk work is necessary because when you arrive in the field, you must be ready. Ready to go, ready to roll, ready to hit the ground running. You can't do "desk work" on the ground—that is called "field" work. Woe to the consultant who is not ready! In the field, you will have so many other issues to deal with—and the time for desk work will be a distant, hazy memory.

So, how do I prepare? When an organization sends me documents to review or to familiarize myself with, that is a great help, but reading those is really only opening the door. I am paid the same rate at home as I am on the road, and I use the time in a similar way. I need to show up ready. Readiness and preparation start way before the flight. But it often feels like I am riding the whirlwind, as soon as I get a contract. I begin the immersion, the prep work, which culminates in the training that is delivered, and doesn't end until after I have completed my report back home. (The report writing time is sometimes also called desk work). So, even though I'm jetlagged, wicked tired, high from a post-training success or disoriented from an unexpected challenge, I have to stay in the moment, the mind, of that project, until the contract is completed.

While each country and project is different, essentially my philosophy about preparation boils down to this idea: "*Implementing family therapy training in a state that is not one's home country is best completed after gathering information about the lives of the people you are expected to train, including their personal, family, and gender security (human security)*" (Charlés, 2015). This information is directly related to their access to and definition of acceptable types of mental health work, and also, of course, the nature of what it means to work with families in that place.

In the kind of multilateral work I do, it has been useful to understand how labor in mental health and psychosocial health is distributed across different sectors and groups, particularly for those trainees or beneficiaries (to use the development terminology) that are targeted in the training I am about to give. Who are they? How were they identified? What is their role and in what setting? How is your training a part of a larger initiative (if it is, at all) to scale up mental health services in a country? Who supports these initiatives? Financially? Morally? Internationally as well as in country? Regionally? Who is not supporting it?

I rarely have a say in any of these matters, but that is not the point. As in a family session, it helps for me to understand the relationships between the people/partners involved. I need that so that I can best organize my frame, to better deliver a training that is consistent with and matches the needs on the ground. I need that to help me to do something that can be sustained, and meaningful.

I have learned to choose carefully how I organize my learning, my analysis, my sources of understanding. I might pull country reports from the International Crisis Group, or Human Rights Watch, if what I am working on is in their area of expertise. It often is. I find each of these group's reports very useful and consistent with what I learn on the ground with actual people living in the context of that particular report. In fact, I have later met some of the authors of these reports in my work in the country, which has been such a wonderful surprise. So now, after certain projects, I have a definite go-to person in those contexts. I know I can count on their work to help make sense of my own.

I might read things about the country, or the region, searching particularly for information about its governance and leadership, or its public institutions (like health and education). I might look at its economy, its foreign direct investment or humanitarian aid and trade (who is paying for this project, and how is it going to continue?) There is unlikely to be much literature on mental health in that country (although I can always count on the MH Atlas published by WHO). Thus, reading on the periphery of mental health in that country or region is required; I need to do a type of triangulation (the qualitative research kind, not the Bowenian kind).

I am essentially doing a macro-analysis of the context, as a way to inform the micro-analysis of my work in the country. And then, like Jay Haley once said, I take all that I learned theoretically with me until I meet the people on the ground. Then, I leave it at the door and start the process of learning all over again, by and through my interactions with people in the setting. Sometimes, what I had read before is very helpful; sometimes, it is not. Usually, I am grateful to have it as background. It comes in handy, but usually, not in the way I expect.

In multilateral work, countries are often a focus but areas of content are also a way to focus. In other words, "presenting problems" that a family might have are also parallel in a way to the country level. There are particular arenas, issues, challenges, that are common across countries. For example, countries that were once in the midst of armed conflict, but now are not, may be dealing with issues specific to transitional justice. I have inadvertently found myself immersed in these matters, simply because of the regions where I have worked. As a consequence, I have become comfortable working in the arena of transitional justice, having spent so much time in post-conflict settings, which by their nature are focused on issues of reconciliation and reconstruction of society after war.

To enhance my learning, I then take all this further, often immersing in literature and critical contemporary questions about the topic from as many angles as I can read. When I do say 'Yes', however, it is always with the framing question of "What do I do to develop my proficiency in a content area (or state condition or historical or cultural meaning) that is new to me?" (Charlés and Bava, 2020).

I have found it so useful to inhabit a type of professional multi-tasking that is dynamic and unpredictable at every level in order to do this work. I cannot be one-dimensional; I cannot allow myself to be used to one way of behaving. As systemic practitioners, we are always conscientious of our relationships with people, the effects of our responses on their work and the future of their work, and live with an agility that comes from attending to people moment to moment. We thrive inside the complexity, which is always an important message for us about the local knowledge, and how we are negotiating it. This is true in multilateral work as well; it is a useful, necessary construct to hold on to.

References

Charlés, L. L. (2015). Scaling up family therapy in fragile, conflict-affected states. *Family Process, 54* (3), 545–558.

Charlés, L. & Bava, S. (2020). *"Family therapy & Global mental health: Reflections on professional development and training."* In M. Rastogi & R. Singhe (Volume Editors), K. Wampler (Series Editor), *Handbook of systemic family therapy*, Volume IV. New York: Wiley.

Charlés, L. & Piercy, F. P. (2003). Reflections on teaching family therapy in several non-Western countries. *Journal of Systemic Therapies*, 22 (4), 15–28.

Piercy, F. (1998). An American family therapist teaches in Indonesia: A collage [Special Issue: Consulting and Training in the Land of Others]. *Journal of Systemic Therapies*, 17, 69–81.

Ungar, M. (2003) Lessons on "Otherness": What therapists can learn from traveling. *Journal of Systemic Therapies*, 22 (4), 1–14.

13

SAFETY AND RISK MITIGATION

At Home and in the Field

Danger at the border: Urgent. Your team of two is returning to country X after a day working in the northern region of nearby Country Z. Traveling by private car, your small NGO team is interrogated at the border between the two countries at dusk. The border closes at 5 p.m. and the crossing is in an isolated, dangerous zone between the two countries. As a woman, you are at risk of sexual assault if you stay here. As you stand together in the small room where an officer examines your passports, your NGO contact person begins to argue with the authorities. The arguing between them ends when a uniformed authority points his finger in another direction and states you must walk one mile, "in that direction," to meet the head of the local government committee.

Following are the key facts about your current situation:

(1) You are a family therapy consultant from the U.S., hired to work with an NGO based in the high-income nation of Country Y, but working in the region of their project in Country X for several weeks.

(2) The NGO has people on the ground; however, they are in the capital city of Country X, and you cannot reach them. Your contact and team member in the private vehicle, also from the NGO, is familiar with the region and very competent.

(3) You and your team member both speak the primary languages of this region and you both have equal time in terms of your background working in region. However, your counterpart seems to be upsetting the authorities rather than assuaging them and you are quite surprised by the behavior at the border.

(4) You feel you are at risk and need to identify ways to decrease risk. What do you do first? What do you do next? Name the steps you would take in order you would take them. Describe your reasoning. Who is critical for you to speak with? To refrain from speaking to? How do you prioritize? Explain. What more data do you need to know to deal with this situation? Do you have the time to find out, given the danger/security issues? What data do you prioritize at this point?

I handed this scenario to a class of doctoral students in a course I taught in global humanitarian mental health at Our Lady of the Lake University a few years ago. We spent the next couple of hours sorting through the issues of safety and security. As with any seasoned clinician's work, it is part of the equation to deal with crises and potential for harm in one way or another. We are trained how to manage life-threatening situations, and how to analyze and act on our ethical and professional responsibilities therein. Yet, this training may be insufficient when working internationally, multilaterally, and in global settings. Sometimes, as in a pandemic, the global emergency comes to us, and we are forced to think of safety and how to mitigate threats that seemed at one time irrelevant.

The way to think about risk and security needs to be expanded when one is working multilaterally. For instance, disappearances, forced displacement, or torture, are quite common matters for citizens in many countries. Fear or distrust of the government can inhibit citizens' responses to emergencies, and exacerbate their own risk. Even high-income countries and liberal, consolidated democracies can find themselves in the middle of a humanitarian emergency, such as a pandemic, which will put into stark relief the gaps in human security citizens face. Clinicians and consultants may indeed find themselves facing similar problems that their clients face. In other words, terrible things do not happen only to clients; of course, they can happen to us, too.

I had a very harsh awakening to the implications of this awareness when I worked in one country, Country A, a few years ago. In my experience up to that time, most clinicians in international organizations or funded via initiatives on the international plane, would not refer out these clients who had been tortured, or were seeking asylum. In my work in the U.S., for example, many of my students over the years desired clinical internships and experience working at torture treatment centers. In Country A, however, a country where state torture is practiced against those who speak out against the government, my family therapy trainees had been quite understandably uninterested in making a career working with torture survivors. Most of them were young women, yet to be married, thus with very little status in the community. In one of the most terrible of ironies, they would be putting themselves at risk in fact, when working with this population. Risk is relative. It is dependent on context, of course. Context, in multilateral work, includes the social, economic, and diplomatic efforts being made to mitigate that risk.

In case you did not guess, I had been the woman in the brief scenario I'd given the doctoral students. Years earlier, I had taken part in a similar exercise in Budapest, Hungary, in a training course on international security studies. The context of that crisis exercise was the bombing at Hotel Mumbai. In our exercise, our "teams" —my fellow classmates— had to address similar questions as posed above.

It was realistic, and powerful, to see the dynamics of our team unfold, each of us having different ideas about what to do first. Here, in the humanitarian class at OLLU, I realized I actually had my own Hotel Mumbai moment. Indeed, I had not forgotten it, but I'd not quite seen how useful it could be as a training exercise for family therapists interested in international work. Although I have worked in some very dangerous areas, I think it is interesting and worth some thought that I have very rarely felt in danger or at risk in these places that are considered risky. The danger is always so much more prescient for host country nationals, in my view. And I am always the one who gets on the plane to leave at the end. Right?

My feelings about risk and danger have changed somewhat since I became more involved as a family therapy consultant to a United Nations/WHO psychotherapeutic interventions training projects. The Boston Marathon Bombing occurred in the days that I was finalizing the terms of reference for one of those contracts, which would eventually take me to Libya as a family therapy trainer. At the time the bombs went off, I was at home, working. I had been to the gym that morning, and remember I had watched a bit of the marathon on the TV while running on a treadmill.

When the news of the bombing broke on my computer screen, at home a few hours later, I quickly messaged my spouse. He had been working that day, at one of the hospitals in Boston. I told him to get home as soon as possible, as I suspected the MBTA (Massachusetts Bay Transit Authority) system would close and the city would be locked down as the search for the suspects, and perhaps other bombs, continued. He had not heard the news of the bombing, but did manage get on the train before the lockdown and arrived home safely a few hours later. We had had a plan for this kind of "extraction" when we lived in Cairo; that's how we already knew what to do. We of course had never expected to use it in Boston.

A few minutes after I'd messaged him, I remember that I began to get personal messages from across the globe via various messaging apps. The one I remember most clearly was from a UN colleague in North Africa, the very person with whom I was negotiating the contract to Libya. My colleague wrote something like this, from Tripoli: "*I am following the sad news, and feeling very sorry to see this, my heart and prayers with you, your friends and family. Hope you all are safe.*" From Libya, in that time, in those two moments, his words brought me to a stark realization: Today, it feels like Libya is safer than Boston. Risk is relative.

As I heard once in a family therapy risk management training, "Risk is always present. Your goal should be to minimize risk—you can't eliminate it." So rather than opine on risk here or risk there, or chastise those who call me brave (something I don't like very much), I have tried to remain cold and methodical when it comes to assessing risk, and in how to take the steps I can to minimize it. Human security is an everyday challenge for most people in the world. In what should be no surprise, I've learned a great deal from the people I work with in countries around the globe.

The Central African Republic. Syria. The Democratic Republic of Congo. Cairo. Libya. Beirut. Sri Lanka. Cameroon. Kosovo. In the last few years, I have worked with people in places that make the news every day. Yet all kinds of families live in these places, and the everyday business of living happens for them. They work and go to school. They get married; they have children. They pray; they mourn. They plan for the future. Sometimes, bombs are falling in their neighborhood. Sometimes, they are in quarantine, separated from their family members at the time they need them the most.

Of the different types of human security issues I have to think about, I think the easiest to plan for is the physical security. Two of the things I do first when invited to a project in a new country are 1. Talk to someone who has lived/worked there; and 2. Download analyses of various situation reports in the country—particularly analyses that focus on the country's status and conditions. I am figuratively mindful that the map is not the territory, but literally, before I go to the field and assess it, I am also mindful that it helps so much to have a confident glimpse of the map in the first place.

The map/territory analysis is a dynamic process. Security is a fluid issue in many of the places I work, certainly around world and across communities. One day, things are relatively safe. The next, the airport is closed due to militias in combat with each other. The changes only *appear* to happen overnight. But they don't. There is a logic to them. That is why it is important to learn what is happening on the ground *right now*—from people who are in the field, or through analyses from organizations with people on the ground. One of the reasons it was so easy for me to go to Libya, in fact, and although I knew so little about the context, was because of the trust I had with my contact there, as a person, and as a professional.

I do other things for security, too. For communications when I travel, I often take multiple phones, both a smart phone and a dumb phone, including my Blackberry, which is my preferred phone, unlocked. If it is feasible and necessary, I obtain a SIM in the new place—particularly if I am staying more than two weeks. (Sometimes I am given a local phone to use while in country, but not always).

If I am working outside my home country, I sometimes use an internet phone number, with a U.S. area code, so my family can call me at any time and leave a message. Even if I am unable to answer, they can reach me; they can at least feel like I am accessible. I used to be careful with my iPhone when traveling, but now, I am more thoughtful about its storage, and its content. I am often questioned very thoroughly after I arrive home from a place, and my passport contains stamps from several countries that are considered risky to travel to. I am often asked: *What were you doing in* _____? *How did that go? Do you plan to return?* I have been questioned many, many times, about the kind of work I do as well as the kind of places I travel. It is not always pleasant, but I wear a cheerful face, anyway. I want it to be easy.

I always keep a paper copy of my contract with me. It is reassuring to carry this because although I can and will certainly verbalize what my project and TOR (Terms of Reference) is all about—I am also likely to be quite tired, jetlagged, and disoriented when I am questioned. Crossing a border can be stressful, and exhausting, and confusing. I make it easy on myself and on the persons who inevitably will question me about why I am in Libya? Uzbekistan? Bangui? It helps to show them a piece of paper, and to let that speak for me, if necessary.

There are a few things I do when I travel far away. Several years ago, we deliberately chose a very specific type of credit card, because of the benefits I might need during travel. For me, one of these includes emergency evacuation from a country if needed. Fortunately, I have never had to use this and I have discovered if I choose projects correctly, I will probably never need to. As one of my contacts said, when we were working in another MENA (Middle East/North Africa) country, "*Laurie, trust me, if we have to get you out of the country, we will get you out.*" They were very reassuring. However, I had to laugh because they also said if I was kidnapped the project would go bankrupt, and they were absolutely not going to let that happen. So, in a way, they were focused on minimizing risk as well.

It might not be clear until literally the night before I get on the plane that I find out where I am staying. When I find out, I write those phone numbers down somewhere, both to leave at home and also to carry in my wallet. I am likely also to send them in a text to one family member, who organizes a "text tree" to everyone else who is on a needs-to-know-basis. These days it is easy to keep people informed. But I am not a tourist in these places; I am not going to publicize everything I do. I use social media but I am likely to be quite circumspect about what and when I post for others to see.

When I arrive in a place, I am usually very jetlagged, tired, and irritable (or worse, disoriented and giddy)—and usually do not have the cognitive abilities to search out a new phone number anywhere but my pocket. As I said, I carry my paper contract with me at all times on my person, in case I ever need to explain or prove to someone what I am doing in the country. I've only had to show this once, and it was upon my return to the U.S. I carry a copy of my passport in more than one place; my family also has a copy in case it is needed. If the country I am going to has required me to get a visa, I copy those, too, and leave a copy at home. Depending on what country I am in, I may carry my passport on my person. Sometimes, it is safe enough where I am to leave in the hotel safe, or in a locked compartment of some kind where I am staying.

I do my best to mitigate risk but of course, things do happen, everywhere. Risk is relative; risk is part of living. I've been burgled in Asia; I've been mugged in East Africa. Always, when something not so great has happened in a project where I am working, I have been able to rely on the kindness of friends and colleagues in the host country.

The person who mugged me came at me in the hard, cold light of day, and he didn't get very far after he took my bag. Numerous bystanders chased him down and he was quickly arrested. When we were burgled, a colleague at the Fulbright office in Colombo saw our distress, and unbeknownst to us, asked a friend of his who was going to Scotland for six months to rent us his Colombo flat during that time. He could have left his beautiful flat empty, but he didn't. The fact that he let us the flat, however, was probably key to our ongoing infatuation with that country. It was very Sri Lankan to do that, I think. The flat was a beautiful penthouse, with a rooftop garden that allowed us to watch the green parakeets sweep past the trees every evening at dusk. What could have been the end of our feeling of goodwill for a place ended up being the beginning.

In the moments I am in the company of very seasoned people in the international relations field, I am of course tempted to ask them their thoughts about safety and security. What are their own best practices? What tried and true methods do they use? How do they think about it all? I have learned things from such seasoned folks, and added them to my own routines in more than one case.

However, when I'm asked the same questions, I am always unsure what to say. I do not feel I have any answers, no magic formula. There are indeed practices, typical actions I take "on the road." I often use the same practices at home, too. That is one suggestion I am mindful to share with folks. "Use your own best practices; add to them as needed." There have been critical modules and preparation guides I've been lucky enough to draw from across projects. It is worthwhile to take advantage of modules offered by the organization or project with which you are engaged.

Briefings and debriefings are also useful. What is discussed or brought to the fore in those discussions is likely to be contextual, however. There are aspects of identity (whether it is the organization one works for, or one's gender identity or color of one's passport or one's native language or clothing) that mean different things in different places. To assess that meaning, one must learn about the context of a place, and the context within a certain moment. That means one requires access to information that is relevant on the ground, that is, "in the territory." Yet, I also think the issue of safety and security is deeply personal. We do not all share the same tolerance for risk; we do not all see danger in the same way. We are part of the equation, too.

14

LEADING FROM THE EDGE AND LEADING FROM THE CENTER

Working in International Teams

My work as an international subject matter expert in family therapy increased dramatically after my graduation from the Fletcher School of Law and Diplomacy. At the time, I was already a mid-career professional, established as a scholar with pieces published in the Journal of Marital and Family Therapy, Family Process, and the Journal of Family Therapy; and a healthy CV full of presentations I'd done, at what I had felt were all of the important family therapy conference venues. I'd held various positions as both faculty member and as a program leader; I'd done a Fulbright. Trainees recognized my name at conferences, and academic colleagues expressed interest in working alongside me.

Nevertheless, I did not think very much about leadership, and what it meant in the work I was doing. If anything, I felt on the periphery of leadership, at least in the field of family therapy. I still do. Yet, a few years post-Fletcher, and about a dozen country projects after that degree, I think about leadership very differently. Today, I see it everywhere. It is front and center in the kind of work I do.

There are so many dimensions to leadership. However, in international affairs specific to my work with supporting families' needs in the context of global mental health and psychosocial support, there are particular patterns that repeat themselves year after year, project after project. First: I tend to work a great deal in conflict zones. Like Paul Collier (2018) said, conflicts are the most awful things that can happen in a country. So, I am often in settings where the worst things have happened, or are happening, to the people with whom I am going to work. I need to work effectively alone as well as in a team, with people I've never met, and who are also multinational and multilingual. The context of constant crises forges leadership skills in people who survive it.

Second, the people I work with in these countries—usually I am delivering a training of some kind—are a mixture of host country nationals who are often leaders in their own right, or perhaps on the cusp of leadership themselves. Typically, they are also quite enthusiastic, and seem full of gratitude for my presence on the ground. They are also quite capable in ways that surpass my own experience. Surely, my education and background add credibility to what I do: that is the "expert" part of subject matter expert, and people respond positively to that. However, there is so much more required in leadership, and I find that it is as subtle and nuanced as well as declarative. When I am focused on noticing others' leadership qualities in my own international work, especially those of trainees I meet, I find I use both kinds of leading, from the edge and from the center.

In a project in Libya in 2013 and 2014, I was struck by how the numerous males in a psychotherapeutic training course I was delivering for the World Health Organization seemed to look up to me and admire me. The women in the course seemed to as well—they often touched my hand, my arm, to express their admiration, and in private, giggled and hugged me in the company of the other women, but not in the company of the men.

With the males, equal in number to the females, admiration was also there, but it was communicated differently. Gender roles precluded them expressing admiration in the ways the women had; instead, they went out of their way to talk to me, to ask questions, or to take photos with me, with a respectable distance between our private/public space. They were fearless about looking me in the eye to thank me profusely for what I was doing.

One night after our training, when our team was relaxing at the Radisson Blu in Tripoli, I wondered aloud to one of my peers in the project—the other consultants, the WHO affiliates—all males—how it was that the men seemed so engaged with me? One of them, wisely making note of the era of Qadaffi that had preceded the project, suggested, "*They are learning from you, that's why they look up to you.*" Sometimes leadership is just showing up. Or at least, showing up at the right time.

However, even when I "show up," I am typically on the ground for only a brief set of days, in this place where the worst things are happening. That brings me to the third thing. I must also work to read and act within the kaleidoscope of the geopolitical landscape in front of me. If not, I risk its poor outcome. I always want to be acting in such a way as to mitigate that risk. I have found that paying heed to the kaleidoscopic realities, a 360–degree lens that I learned as a student at the Fletcher School, makes my work more efficient and more sustainable.

I've learned it's a test of leadership to act conversely to expectations. Once, I was sent to work in Damascus—and, unable to cross the border from Lebanon, I found myself expected to achieve the project outcome while sidelined in Beirut. What, then? Leadership forged in experiences in crisis or war (even vicariously as mine has been) really hones an ability to act contrary to expectations. When things don't go how they are supposed to, I have learned to see advantages in the alternatives laid out before me. I have the confidence and strategy I need to act on them. I don't mind it at all. Rather, I have *learned* not to mind it.

Whether I find myself leading from the edge or leading from the center, in Beirut when I should be in Damascus, I lead myself and I lead with others. I take cues from all the systemic network of players in my midst. There is so much talent on the ground! Leadership, for me, is the capacity to tap into the talent that is there—by showing up, by acting decisively before the alternatives laid out in front of me, by making assets of problems, and sometimes even acting contrary to expectations. My goal is to deliver whatever I can to help those who can move their country forward, from fragility to stability. The route to sustainability is not always a straight line—rather, it is sometimes circuitous, hidden, and I need to act in an innovative and contrary manner to reach a desired outcome.

Expert Humility as Leadership

In 2011, I was in Sri Lanka working with an international NGO, contracted as a consultant for a capacity building project involving in country psychosocial workers as well as those in the nearby Maldives. I was in the country for 21 days, which was a lovely opportunity after having lived in the country the year before as a Fulbright Scholar. Since then, I have worked, lived, and visited in Sri Lanka numerous times—but back then, the country was still quite new to me. In particular, I knew very little about the relationship between Sri Lanka and the Maldives, a neighboring country of 1,192 islands. Although since that time, I have traveled to and worked in the Maldives, back then, I only knew that the U.S. Embassy in Colombo served both countries.

Towards the end of that 21-day contract, one of the project officers at the NGO heard about my qualitative research background. She approached me and asked if I would be willing to do a brief training for their project staff. The NGO had a project section on governance and civil society capacity building, implemented in the Maldives, where the staff often worked with local communities. I was thrilled to be asked.

When I began the seminar, some days later, I had spoken only a few minutes when the Project Director interrupted me with the following words: *"Please. We are not academics; we are development workers. Can you teach us how to mainstream qualitative research, and which methods we should use in our project, so it is understandable for us?"* At first, I was taken aback by her interruption. As a consultant subject matter expert, I am often seen as "uninterruptible." But, not in Sri Lanka. It is one of the few places I have worked where I feel both useful and unnecessary—appreciated yet also, interruptible.

This NGO has offices throughout all parts of Asia and has been operating for over sixty years. They were the experts in this scenario, whereas I was the outsider, expert or no. At that particular time at that Sri Lanka NGO, I remember how many consultants were there, of every kind, from all over the world. About a dozen of us shared a small suite of cubicles in the back; we traded stories on our work each day. Our number seemed to make us somewhat less unique, less unusual. We were served tea at 10 a.m. and 2 p.m., as was everyone else on the staff.

Accustomed to expert expats, the NGO staff member, of course, had no qualms about redirecting me. This NGO has continued to be one of my best collaborators.

Extreme Leadership and Grand Strategy[1]

In my class on Foreign Policy Leadership at Fletcher, I remember learning something about how leaders "have to be in the wilderness," with plenty of time alone, for reflection. It is said that leaders must read voraciously; not only consuming information but reading in a purposeful way, quite outside their areas of expertise, be it history, politics, economics, or biography. I have found this true in my multilateral work. I have to "leave home" and read voraciously outside my own neighborhood. Paul Theroux also wrote this idea down at a time I needed to hear it: "My advice to any young person who wants to write is: Leave home" (2000).

Not only do we need to be able to "leave home"; leaders must succeed in a new context and get it all down, quickly. We must have the flexibility of mind to be able to understand something new, right away. When I am contracted for an international mission, I do my best to learn quickly what I don't know, and then prepare to learn even more when I am in the territory. I have to leave home and I have to absorb the new place, an instantaneous series of a-ha's, happening over and over.

Leadership is seen as a "soft power" and tends to be dismissed. Leadership, however, is also, of course, "smart power." It is critical across sectors, in public health, in foreign direct investment, in development, in coalition building, in public diplomacy. Smart power becomes critical when the ground begins to liquefy, which sounds ominous, but is part of the story of work on the international plane. Similarly, family therapists working systemically are quite accustomed to liquefied ground in the midst of a family session. There is a symmetry here between how we organize ourselves as clinicians. We are trained to encounter this uncertainty; we are educated to prepare for how to negotiate it.

In multilateral practice as a family therapist, where we are working as partners alongside so many representatives from other countries, we must do what foreign policy leaders do on a regular basis: Negotiate what international relations folks call a two-level game, "balancing [our] own perceived domestic and international pressures, while also simultaneously trying to comprehend the nature of the same balancing act in which [our] counterparts are engaged" (Hermann & Hagan 1998, 134).

According to Gorener and Meltem (2011), the nature of the requirements for international leadership was summarized in questions initially put forth by Hermann and Hagan (1998, p. 363), which I modify here:

(1) Do leaders challenge or respect the constraints in the environment?
(2) Are leaders open or closed to information coming from their environment?
(3) What reasons motivate leaders to seek international work in multilateral, global mental health? Are they driven by a cause, ideology, the desire for power and status or by an interest in building relationships?

Intersectionality and Leadership

One's cultural identities always exist in relation to the belief systems in a society. In that way, categories of identity are not static, but rather, dynamic. Further, identity is shaped by the place and time in which that person has lived, worked, or been educated. In their review of foreign policy leadership, Hermann and Hagan (1998) suggested that "worldviews of leaders are shaped in large part by the generation that they happened to be born into—specifically, by what critical political events they and their cohorts have faced during their lifetimes" (142).

Intersectionality is very useful method of analysis of leadership in multilateral, international affairs. It references in a critical manner how multiple categories of individual identity can be appreciated and evaluated within the context of the society or environment in which they exist. It is a multi-axial method that looks beyond one category, such as gender or race, to understand how the concept of identity can be understood. Hernandez, Almeida, and Dolan-Del Vecchio (2005) defined it thus:

> Intersectionality refers to an analysis of the dynamic interplay of one's gender, race, sexual orientation, age, disability status, and other diversity characteristics upon multiple aspects of one's identity; including

the resources and lack of resources these differences convey upon the individual within their current societal context.

(Hernandez, et al., 2005, p. 106)

Intersectionality is uniquely different depending on the leader's geography, economic status of her state, and belief systems about religion, relationship, and the natural world in her society. This uniqueness is sometimes referenced using the term "social location." Social location—the context in which leaders are raised and brought up and the beliefs associated with that period—allow for various leadership opportunities and roles to come to the fore; it also influences the way we perform leadership. I think about intersectionality as a dynamic, moving thing; it transforms and is both transformed by the international contexts I work in.

From the Margin to the Center

In 2015, I was deployed to Guinea, West Africa as part of the WHO MHPSS response to the 2014 Ebola Virus Disease outbreak. Several weeks into my mission, our team went to Monrovia, Liberia, to join other stakeholders in a meeting on mental health and psychosocial support specific to the regional effects of the West African Ebola Virus Disease outbreak in Guinea, Liberia, and Sierra Leone. The meeting brought together over 75 representatives from the three countries, including members of the Ministries of Health and Social Welfare, national and international NGO partners and donor agencies, in addition to WHO MHPSS staff from Headquarters, the WHO Regional Office for Afica and the three WHO country offices.

The conference was of course interesting to me in so many ways, but one of my first impressions was how outside my team and I felt as participants from Guinea, a French speaking country. Everyone was speaking English, except us. Not even me. We were also a small team; other countries had brought teams of 10 or 15 people, three times our size. I will never forget the excited animated chatter that we were outside of that first night, and how it felt to have everyone walk past us. Everyone seemed to assume we were Francophone and not Anglophone; no one bothered to find out. That evening when our team sat together, alone, at and after dinner; it was clear we belonged to each other. It was also clear we were not part of the larger, informal chatter happening around us in English. In the middle of so much English, to my astonishment and surprise, I found I was as ignored as my Guinéen team members.

Of course, we had official, simultaneous translation for the conference. But as I was told as a family therapy graduate student, and found to be true as an academic in the field, often the best moments at conferences often happen informally, perhaps at dinner or at the conference venue bar. I realized I was going to have to be much more proactive for my team, who were of course, West Africans, unlike me. However, as no one in any of the Anglophone teams spoke French (many of them were U.S. citizens, actually, and not Francophone) and my team didn't speak English, I became an inadvertent simultaneous translator and cultural broker between Francophone and Anglophone EVD teams.

The next morning, waking up determined and assertive, I walked all around the resort where our meeting was held, carting along with me one or two or all of my host country national team everywhere I went. I introduced my team, repeatedly, to everyone enough times until it became clearly apparent that there were language differences. I remember how much I wanted to problematize it, to make it transparent. I counted it as an achievement when the other country team members (expats, Americans, like me, but working in the EVD outbreak in Liberia and Sierra Leone) were inclined to say, "Oh I wish I knew more French!"

I interpreted; I acted as a shadow; I acted as a consultant to the other U.S. folks but also, co-Francophone to my non-U.S. Francophone Guinéens. I wanted us to engage; I wanted the others to notice us, to see us. Even though I had just arrived, I knew my time in Guinea would pass quickly. As an outsider, I was going to leave Guinea. But Ebola was not leaving, nor were my colleagues leaving Africa. I felt I had to make the effort to connect them.

As I wrote at the time:

> For me, the impact on our team (international and national) was huge; partly so because we could see the difference between the countries in terms of resources, which gave some context for us. For one of my counterparts present, it was so helpful to her that another person in Liberia offered ideas on how they could collaborate on women's issues

relevant to effects of Ebola. For her, French speaking only, this was a huge sense of collaboration and camaraderie. That last piece was also part of the morale boost for the team. Guinea is difficult because of the acute situation of Ebola transmission, the lack of budget for mental health, and on the other hand, the intense commitment and motivation of host country nationals working with us and trying so hard to change things. As one told me, 'I feel motivated now! and eager to talk to others so they too become engaged in a national agenda to support the implementation of mental health services.'

(Charlés, as cited in Pearson, 2015)

It is said leaders transform the way people see things. But I think also it's that transformation inspires one's own leadership experience. This is true especially during times of major change. In other words: all the time.

High Complexity Leadership

Situational events can influence the politics and performance of leadership in surprising and unexpected ways (Hermann & Hagan, 1998). Looking at foreign policy and history, for example, Hermann and Hagan (ibid.) noted how much Anwar el Sadat changed his previous foreign policy by traveling to Jerusalem, how much Yitzhak Rabin changed by pursuing the Oslo accords, and similarly, how much Richard Nixon changed when he began opening relations with China. Hermann and Hagan summarized these cases thus:

Arguments abound as to whether these leaders themselves changed or whether they were merely responding to changes in the international scene, their domestic arenas, or perceived opportunities to attain goals that might previously have been foreclosed to others. Underlying this debate is the question concerning the extent to which leaders shape their own preferences.

(ibid., p. 142)

Our social location and intersectional identities can prepare us well for leadership on the domestic arena, but not always the radically changing international one (Yoder, 2011). Many leaders on the international stage may have a lack of experience in world affairs; perhaps they have not traveled very much, nor worked in countries outside their own. This can result in what Dyson (2009) identified as a cognitive style of processing information that illustrates "a profoundly "black-and-white" view of international affairs" (ibid., p. 34). However, successful leaders find ways to overcome a lack of international experience and any deficits in content and relational knowledge about a multi-polar global order. One way they can do that is through their choice of advisors, who may fill in the gaps in understanding and knowledge.

Leaders must have the strength of character and presence of mind to surround themselves with a set of learned advisors, including those learned in areas where they are not. According to Dyson (ibid.), high complexity leaders are those who value opinions and input that challenge their own views, who actively solicit dissent from others they trust. In a sense, leaders use these contrary experts and advisors as a kind know-ledge transfer. I like this idea of high-complexity leaders. It reminds me as well of the nature of systemic work, and the nature of communication.

I often find I am working in international teams that are beyond any complexity I could have imagined in my training. This is remarkable to me, as someone who has served in the Peace Corps, as someone who traveled as part of a cast of 100+ multi-country international singing group at the age of 19. My work in teams today, for instance, is routinely multilingual, even polylingual. I have become accustomed to working with multiple interpreters at the same time, which is a given in the contexts where I train.

Working inside multilateral projects and organizations means I also work across a range of consolidated and unconsolidated democracies, and with trainees who are living inside them. That is, they are living with a different set of liberties and constraints from those that I live in—and also, from each other. That is because most trainings I do now involve citizens from five or six countries at the same time.

Multilateral leadership also requires a mastery of relational inter-action with others. In addition to the differences across states and states' norms, our colleagues in multilateral projects may embody personality characteristics, lived experiences, and social identities that are contrary, or anathema to us. Leadership in the realm of multilateral work as a family therapist requires an ability to operate theoretically and practically between both possibilities and their limitations, and in real time engagement with other people—who may not, cannot, or will not necessarily operate the same way.

For many years I did this work alone, as a sole trainer or consultant. However, in the last five years I am always part of an international set of trainers, working as a team. Except for a possible Skype call beforehand, I don't usually meet my team until I am actually on the ground. Each of these conditions adds a layer of complexity to leadership that is often unexpected for me. At the same time, it is fascinating to experience. It can lay the ground for so much future relational collaboration.

Systemic family therapy work in multilateral projects is a kind of diplomacy and leadership that requires the ability to engage across borders in effective and sometimes unexpected ways. Leadership skills honed at home, in one's comfortable context of familiarity, is only part of the equation. The other part is what is on the other side of "home," whether it is the language, geography, or state characteristics. Engagement across divergent landscapes is critical for work in international teams. Yet, it is the capacity to lead them, in the front or at the back, from the margin or the center that matters in a multipolar world. We cannot afford to be isolationist in our approach to leadership. In order to grow as a professional, we must leave home.

Note

1 Dean Deborah Nutter at the Fletcher School was the first to introduce to me the idea of foreign policy leadership as extreme leadership.

References

Collier, P. (April 16, 2018). Roundtable on state fragility and development. *Spring meetings of the International Monetary Fund (IMF) and the World Bank Group*. Washington D.C.

Dyson, S. B. (2009). Cognitive style and foreign policy: Margaret Thatcher's black and white thinking. *International Political science review, 30* (1), 33–48.

Gorener, A. S. & Meltem, U.S. (2011). The personality and leadership style of Recep Tayyip: Implications for Turkish foreign policy. *Turkish Studies, 12* (2), 358–381.

Hermann, M. G. & Hagan, J. D. (1998) International decision making: Leadership matters, *Foreign Policy, Special Edition: Frontiers of Knowledge (Spring, 1998)*, 110, 124–137.

Hernandez, P. Almeida, R., & Dolan-Del Vecchio, K. (2005). Critical consciousness, accountability, and empowerment: Key processes for helping families heal. *Family Process, 44*, 105–119.

Pearson, H. (2015) Building back better from West Africa's Ebola outbreak. *Mental Health Innovation Network: A Global Community of Mental Health Innovators*. Accessed at www.mhinnovation.net/blog/2015/jun/24/building-back-better-west-africa%E2%80%99s-ebola-outbreak?mode=List

Theroux, P. (2000). *Fresh Air Fiend: Travel Writings 1985–2000*. New York: Houghton Mifflin.

Yoder, J. (2011). An intersectional approach to Angela Merkel's foreign policy. *German Politics, 20* (3), 360–375.

15

TRAINING THE NEXT GENERATION OF SKILLED INTERNATIONAL FAMILY THERAPIST

Laurie L. Charlés, Florence Lewis, Dorcas Matowe, Melissa Yzaguirre and Safia Jama

For this chapter, I, Laurie, consulted with four newly trained family therapy professionals who I met and worked with over the past two years in my role as mentor in the AAMFT MFP.[1] Many of the conversations I have shared over the previous few years with my co-authors in this chapter seemed also to comment, in a number of interesting ways, on international aspects of family therapy training. In this chapter, I've asked my colleagues to share some of their experiences and collective ideas about the gap between "what we know, what we don't know, and what we need to know" when it comes to international work as a family therapist. I am grateful for the reminders they bring about what is important about our field. For the purpose of this chapter, each author's contribution will be identified by their first name.

Who We Are and Where We Are

Florence Lewis, Ph.D. holds a doctorate in Medical Family Therapy from East Carolina University, Greenville, North Carolina. She completed her dissertation on addressing the behavioral health needs of displaced families in primary health care settings and is currently living in Northern Italy. As a two-time recipient of the SAMHSA Minority Fellowship, Dr. Lewis's written works include analyses of using African American cultural values to improve health outcomes; supporting immigrant families through the U.S. naturalization process; and exploring the mental health needs of foreign-born U.S. military servicemembers. Dr. Lewis identifies as an African American female, born in the U.S. by an immigrant parent from Sierra Leone, West Africa. Clinically, Dr. Lewis is a bilingual (Spanish and English) family therapist who has served families from various ethnic, racial, and socioeconomic backgrounds.

Dorcas Matowe, Ph.D. LMFT holds a doctorate in Family Therapy from Nova Southeastern University in Fort Lauderdale, Florida. She is an AAMFT Clinical Fellow, Approved AAMFT Supervisor, and a Florida Licensed marriage and family therapist. As a two-time recipient of the SAMHSA Minority Fellowship, Dr. Matowe has conducted research on the prevalence of racial and ethnic health disparities in the U.S. and served on the board of the Broward Association of Marriage and Family Therapy in Fort Lauderdale, Florida. Her perspectives on training the international family therapist include personal and professional experiences of living in the U.S. and Zimbabwe. Dr. Matowe is currently a Clinical Postdoctoral Fellow at The Family Institute at Northwestern University in Evanston, Illinois.

Melissa Yzaguirre is a second-generation Mexican-American who holds a master's degree in Marriage and Family Therapy from the University of Nevada, Las Vegas. She is currently a doctoral student in the Couple and Family Therapy Program in the Department of Human Development and Family Studies at Michigan State University. A first-generation college student, Melissa is a two-time recipient of the SAMHSA Minority Fellowship. Melissa's research includes mental health disparities in ethnic and racial minority populations, specifically Spanish-speaking populations in the U.S. Melissa served on the Diversity,

Equity, and Inclusion steering committee appointed by the Office of the President at Michigan State University to collaborate with different university stakeholders to foster shared values and facilitate an inclusive campus environment.

Safia Jama, B.S. is a third-year master's student in Lewis and Clark University's Marriage and Family Therapy program in Portland, Oregon. She is a two-time recipient of the SAMHSA Minority Fellowship. With a desire to gain experience working internationally, she traveled to Rwanda for a month in 2019 to work with a program that focused on healing trauma in communities that have experienced genocide, high rates of HIV, and conflict. Ms. Jama identifies as a half Somali and half white European female, she is the daughter of a Somali immigrant father. She has focused her studies on substance use disorder while interning as a child and family therapist at a community mental health agency.

Following includes commentary and reflections from all of us, organized with subheadings that evolved from our writing process for this chapter in the Spring of 2020. We present these views in the first person, and in the spirit of the future, to which we all belong, and in response to Laurie's question: How can we best prepare ourselves and each other and our field to work internationally?

We Are Mindful of the Interdisciplinary Nature of Systemic Work

We need more of a "how to" in training settings on interdisciplinary work as international family therapists. In my (Florence) experience, it has always been beneficial to collaborate with other professionals as a way to support the overall needs of clients. Being able to effectively collaborate and work with other professionals is crucially important. As the proverb says, "if you want to go fast, go alone; if you want to go far, go together." In my work, collaboration has included mental health professionals from other behavioral health fields, health care workers, community workers, school staff, and faith leaders. Building a support network for clients and their families rooted within the communities they live in has been at the forefront as I have worked with clients. For the immigrant families I've worked with, this includes making sure that there are resources that are fitting for clients from other countries.

In order to work with other professionals effectively and efficiently, I've had to be secure in my role as a systems thinker and my professional identity while remaining open to new ideas and perspectives. Since many of the clients I've served have been people of color, immigrants, and/or multilingual, the providers and professionals that I've collaborated with have also tended to be people of color, immigrants, multilingual, and/or different from me. I feel fortunate to have been exposed to such a wealth of experience and perspective that has really seasoned my clinical work for the better. Interdisciplinary work is a real "systemic" dance that our training predisposes us, as family therapists, to be able to navigate effortlessly. Additionally, since family therapy is such a small field, the topic of collaboration is particularly important because part of building and maintaining credibility as a field is sustaining dependable relationships with other professionals.

In my (Dorcas) research on racial and ethnic health disparities, I've found that public health takes the lead in global health issues and has laid the foundation for what other health professionals can do to promote awareness of these issues. It therefore makes sense that family therapists should collaborate with public health professionals to succeed in global work. For me, a critical aspect of understanding clients' needs and knowing what supports to put in place is familiarity with factors that contribute to poor health for clients. For example, the social determinants of health (SDOH) are a globally used tool to assess what social, political, and environmental factors create and maintain poor health conditions for communities. However, in my dissertation research conducted with marriage and family therapists (MFTs) in the U.S. (Matowe, 2019), results indicated that 23% of MFTs nationwide were extremely familiar with SDOHs, 33% were moderately familiar, and 26% were somewhat familiar. The Core Competencies of the Commission on Accreditation for Marriage and Family Therapy Education (COAMFTE) do not address SDOHs, thus MFTs' capacity in this area is lacking.

I also believe that to work competently as an MFT on a global scale, trainees should know what kinds of neighborhoods their clients come from and work in. Are they safe or unsafe? Do they have sidewalks or not? Are their neighborhoods saturated with liquor stores and corner stores with a lack of health food stores or farmers markets? Do their clients have access to other necessities like healthcare, adequate employment, running water?

To agree and continue to punctuate Dorcas's points, I, Florence, do believe that one major step in advancing the work of international family therapists is to blend in many of the major tendons of the public health field like SDOHs. As quoted from one of my public health professors, "what is local, is global and what is global, is local." As a systems thinker and clinician, there have been numerous occasions when I was compelled to incorporate public health principles like SDOHs and integrate levels of prevention into my treatment plans particularly for clients who I knew were at risk of poor health outcomes.

My (Florence) experience as a medical family therapist has helped quite a bit with this interdisciplinary work, but I think there needs to be more of an effort on this front in the field overall. Holistic advocacy for clients as an international family therapist includes multiple aspects of health (psychological, social, physical, environmental, etc.) that really lends the advocacy to public health concepts and theory integration. Therefore, the interdisciplinary nature of our work is an area that could be discussed further with skill development as part of training programs' curriculums.

We Recognize the Need for Fluency in Globalization and Its Impacts

I'm realizing more and more how I, Florence, need to work transnationally with my clients. If I were asked two years ago where I would be living now, I never would have thought I would be in Northern Italy, where I now reside. I am trying to orient myself to a new country while my graduate-level education as a family therapist only prepared me to work within the U.S.

When I was in the U.S., so many of my clients had families abroad, even those without an immediate, immigrant background themselves. People are moving around and living all around the world for a wealth of reasons. I think that it is extremely important that we, international family therapists, have tools and resources on hand to begin to unify our systems knowledge with the demands of our rapidly changing world. In addition, there are various challenges that present themselves through the immigrating experience.

I, Dorcas, would also add here to Florence's points that in the training of international family therapists, the challenges of immigrating, including the processes of assimilation and acculturation, should be discussed.

Therapists who are international students coming to the United States to obtain their degree are expected to align with the U.S. education system (Roberts, et al., 2014). One example of this is an experience I, Melissa, shared with a colleague from a continent outside North America in our doctoral diversity course the first year of our program. The instructor had started a discussion about ethnic and racial minority populations. My colleague leaned to me and asked, "What does she [the instructor] mean when she says minority"?

At first, I assumed they were joking, but my colleague went on to explain how much of the terminology used in the U.S. is not used "back home" (in my colleague's country of origin). They informed me that in their country one is either "Domestic" or "International"—that is it. I began to wonder, for therapists coming to the U.S. from other countries with different ways of defining racial and ethnic diversity, what types of situations similar to this one do they face? How are programs taking these thoughts into consideration and incorporating different perspectives into their curriculums?

Additionally, a constant concern I, Melissa, face when working as a therapist and researcher is exploring existing research on my identified population and finding "melting pot" effects within the U.S. Therapists must be mindful of the assumptions or biases held toward different populations based on the labels given to them. This can lead to undesirable outcomes in clinical work, like inaccurate diagnoses or unproductive courses of treatment if treatment is available.

We Believe in the Power of Immersion

For me, Dorcas, it is clear that although theories and interventions can be learned online and, in a classroom, there is no better teacher than immersion, which can help you be present, adaptable, and knowledgeable about the community in which you plan to work. According to McDowell, Goessling, and Melendez (2012), international immersion training builds cultural sensitivity, expands global awareness, demonstrates the significance of culture in all relationships, and provides opportunities for trainees to further assess their knowledge of power and privilege in a global context.

From my (Dorcas) training as a family therapist and through my Zimbabwean-American background, I realize the complexity of international family therapy work as well as the level of fulfillment one receives from such work. My recommendation for any family therapist working internationally is to first become familiar with the political, cultural, and environmental climate of the region in which you choose to work and develop an understanding of how the politics, cultural values, history, and environmental conditions contribute to clients' presenting concerns.

Furthermore, training for family therapists should incorporate training about the values, beliefs, traditions, and rituals of the populations to be served. Family members, especially in collectivist cultures, may question the logic behind individual therapy, talking to an "outsider" about personal issues, and the need to keep therapy conversations confidential.

For example, when I, Dorcas, lived in Zimbabwe and my family was faced with a challenge, we would attempt to resolve the issue as a family, or my parents would plan a meeting with extended family members to discuss solutions. No matter what the problem was, there was never a time that it was dealt with individually; it was always a family issue. Family needs take precedence over individual needs: family members prioritize "we," not "me," and everything they do should be a positive reflection of the family name, from childhood through adulthood. This includes making decisions about future careers and marriage, and providing family support. U.S.-trained family therapists may question such family-focused practices as impinging on individual rights.

We Relentlessly Pursue Diversity, Equity and Inclusion

I, Melissa, have a question to ask the reader: What does diversity mean to you? Who or what constitutes diversity? In many programs today, diversity is forced to fit inside the parameters of one semester or one course. Further, diversity should no longer be limited to race and ethnicity. We miss out on so many communities and identities, leaving us far from competent to work with the populations we continue to exclude.

Along the lines of Melissa's points, in the training programs that I, Dorcas, have attended, the diversity curriculum tended to take on an individually focused approach to psychotherapy training, leaving little room to examine culture beyond the individual and their family of origin. In the diversity course for my doctorate program, one of the assignments required students to identify a population or issue associated with a cultural group that they wanted to learn more about, so it was more about the student's personal and professional growth and less about learning about global issues. This was also the extent of "immersion" in my program; the exposure was limited to one cultural group, which is not typically the case when working internationally.

The emphasis in my program seemed to be on addressing your own discomfort rather than understanding how institutional or national attitudes and policies result in discriminatory action against others. The point here is not to minimize these experiences, but to highlight the absence of systemic thinking on a larger platform. A course on international practice in every FT program would create room for interest in global work, enhance the marketability of the profession, and provide more opportunities for interdisciplinary collaboration. If training programs do not take the lead on global issues, trainees will not either, unless they have a personal interest.

Where Is the Door? As We Find Them, We Will Kick Them Open

As an emerging master's level MFT, I, Safia, find it extremely difficult to find a door that opens to the international work we speak of. I entered my master's program very well knowing that I wanted to work as an international family therapist; however, that felt, and at times still feels, unattainable, as it's hard to know where to even start. As professionals in this field I believe it is important to have the types of discussions we have outlined here. However, we also need to create opportunities within our field, for other emerging MFTs and the next generation of MFTs, to engage in this work early on in their educational journeys.

For instance, as I, Safia, reflect on the communities that we have here in Portland (Somali, Vietnamese, Latinx, etc.) I am reminded how imperative it is for academic programs and other MFT professionals to establish connections with these communities, including elders, professionals, faith leaders, etc. We must do this in order not only to create doors and opportunities for international practitioners but also to engage in inter-disciplinary work while addressing presenting concerns and inequities. I think of the creation of doors like this: these are entryways used to pass through, but more so to hold space to live within the borders of the entryway in order to foster and share growth, knowledge, resources, wisdom, etc. in equitable ways.

As the next generation of family therapists, I, Melissa, think we must continue to be willing to step out of our comfort zones. Therapists can start by asking questions from a curious standpoint with the goal in mind to grow as a person and professional. Therapists hold special skills to help advance the field in a future direction. They can take existing information of different populations and shed light on a new perspective through their experience and knowledge. In order to reach a level of confidence to challenge current discourses, therapists need to be willing to step into a certain level of discomfort. This discomfort will look different for everyone.

If the curriculum within the program you find yourself in does not include your population of interest, it is your responsibility to speak up for yourself and ask for it to be included. At the very minimum, this can turn into a conversation that can take your education to the next level. It may open doors to resources which were not utilized prior to the conversation you, as a future therapist, started.

In order to help therapists learn about owning the many parts of their identity, it is important to understand the meaning of intersectionality with regard to international work.

Early on in their academic career, therapists are exposed to the "self of the therapist" (Aponte et al., 2009). Working on the self of the therapist is a career-long commitment which is forever changing in the different stages of development. Yet, we are not encouraged to self-evaluate through this. We are asked early on to leave parts of ourselves outside the therapy room without realizing the limitations, strains, and confusions this brings for an early therapist. By owning one's identity, adversity, and experiences, we are able to make a larger difference beyond what is taught in any classroom with our clients. It brings our level of internal awareness forward and allows us a meaningful path to connect with others on a deeper level (Aponte & Nelson, 2018).

We Do Believe in Miracles

As a final reflection, we as the authors of this chapter, Laurie, Safia, Melissa, Dorcas, and Florence, asked ourselves the miracle question (de Shazer, 1988). We asked it of ourselves in a way that reflected our hopes for the future of training for international family therapists: If a miracle occurred, overnight while we were sleeping, and all of the family therapy training programs of every kind were now suddenly "expert" in how they trained FTs to work internationally, what would they be doing differently? What are the first three things we would see/notice, that we are not seeing today?

I, Laurie, posted the question on our shared document, and like I once did with a client years ago (Charlés, 2012), let us reflect and stew on the question for several weeks. However, to be quite transparent, I have to say that this is a question I had pondered for a number of years. My answer was fairly quick; I was the first one to respond in the shared document.

Laurie: "My miracle is...."

(1) To require fluency in a second language to graduate, either the language most used in the region of the program, or one of the UN languages required for work as an intern or a consultant/employee.

(2) Doctoral programs would have international internships for students, not as a suggestion but as a requirement; doctoral programs would have these in place and have already done the work to make these happen. This means faculty would have to have international connections that are part of their own work and research, and partnerships and universities would need to provide administrative and financial support and guidance.

(3) Perhaps in master's programs, every university would have a Shoufi Mafi student group like we had at OLLU. Perhaps even with funding by AAMFT.

Dorcas: "I would see...."

(1) A curriculum that highlighted our similarities as human beings. All people, no matter where in the world they are, want the same thing: love, peace, and kindness. If we took this notion across borders, the world would be a much better place.

(2) Education on global health would be a core component of programs so that all trainees graduating from the programs would be well-versed in life on other continents including proficiency on SDoH.

(3) Interdisciplinary and community collaborations as a required element, so family therapists develop the skills needed to work with other professionals and are not fearful of providing service in areas that are different from what they are used to. In this way, every family therapist would understand the impact of racism, discrimination, economic deprivation, abhorrent living and working conditions, societal and institutional policies in maintaining and exacerbating poor health for individuals, families, and communities.

Melissa: "I would see...."

(1) More intentional use of current literature, and teaching family therapists to read/process/and challenge the information they are taking in. I would see trainers and educators be willing to step out of their known areas of interest and explore with their students (side by side) the interest the students hold.

(2) Multilingual therapy would be a norm. This means having bilingual or multilingual therapists blend in as a norm, rather than being the precious gems that are so hard to come by in our field. I would also see this norm be supported by multilingual faculty and supervision easily accessible in the needed language.

(3) I would see more equitable fellowship/scholarships—overall funding in any capacity if we are being honest here—for students who are considered international in the U.S. or looking to work internationally.

Safia: "I would see...."

(1) More coursework offered and available, both required and optional electives, that focus on international training, public health, international relations, culture and community, and international family therapy.

(2) Expanded university collaboration that includes:
   a. University partnerships with local and international communities/universities as well as opportunities for volunteering or potential internships/exchange experiences that focus on international FT.
   b. University interdisciplinary collaboration with other health systems both working and based internationally to provide access to mental health treatment

(3) A designated administrator/faculty or even department that focuses on international therapy. Within this department students would be able to find resources, employment internationally, networking opportunities, information on how to make connections with local immigrant and refugee communities, and assistance with searching for doctoral programs that focus on international therapy.

Florence: "I would see...."

(1) Bilingual supervision options in all programs to help train culturally and linguistically, either in-person or virtually. Multi-language session/training options at national conferences.

(2) International internship options and a virtual job center that posts family jobs around the world for clinical, research, and administrative appointments with resources on how to secure a job overseas and a personal guide to help navigate the visa and licensure process in various countries.

(3) Courses required by COAMFTE on international relations (or something within this arena) and on public health and global mental health (including how diagnosis, assessment, and treatment vary around the world and on alternative healing practices like dance, music, and art).

We are grateful for the opportunity to share our views. We welcome more to this conversation, and all efforts to further family therapy in meaningful, international ways.

Note

1   The authors in this chapter were brought together through the Minority Fellowship Program (MFP) under the American Association for Marriage and Family Therapy (AAMFT) Research and Education Foundation. The MFP is funded through the Substance Abuse and Mental Health Services Administration (SAMHSA) to support masters and doctoral MFT's across the country in their interest in fields of substance abuse and mental health services to minority and underrepresented populations. There are over 500 MFP alumni working in the field of MFT as researchers, instructors, and practitioners. Co-authors SJ, MY, FJ, and DM have all been recipients of this fellowship. This book's author LLC has served as a volunteer mentor for MFP since 2018. The fellowship is a great opportunity for training therapists to learn and grow as professionals, and network with other scholars. Such opportunities are the memorable assets that fuel the next generation of passionate, and skilled, international therapists in our field.

References

Aponte, H. J., & Nelson, G. (2018). "I matter, too." *Journal of Family Psychotherapy: The Person of the Therapist Training (POTT) Model: Theory, Training, and Therapist Personhood, 29* (1), 30–42. doi:10.1080/08975353. 2018.1416232

Aponte, H. J., Powell, F. D., Brooks, S., Watson, M. F., Litzke, C., Lawless, J., & Johnson, E. (2009). Training the person of the therapist in an academic setting. *Journal of Marital and Family Therapy, 35* (4), 381–394. doi:10.1111/ j.1752-0606.2009.00123.x

Charlés, L. (2012). Producing evidence of a miracle: Exemplars of therapy conversation with a survivor of torture. *Family Process, 51,* 25–42.

de Shazer, S. (1988). *Clues: Investigating solutions in brief therapy.* New York: W.W. Norton & Company.

Matowe, D. (2019). Assessing marriage and family therapists' perceptions and knowledge of racial and ethnic health disparities. Unpublished dissertation, Nova Southeastern University, Ft. Lauderdale, FL.

McDowell, T., Goessling, K., & Melendez, T. (2012). Transformative learning through international immersion: Building multicultural competence in family therapy and counseling. *Journal of Marital and Family Therapy, 38* (2), 365–379. doi:10.1111/j.1752-0606.2010.00209.x

Roberts, J., Abu-Baker, K., Diez Fernández, C., Chong Garcia, N., Fredman, G., Kamya, H., ... & Torun Reid, F. (2014). Up close: Family therapy challenges and innovations around the world. *Family process, 53* (3), 544–576.

INDEX

For Product Safety Concerns and Information please contact our EU
representative GPSR@taylorandfrancis.com
Taylor & Francis Verlag GmbH, Kaufingerstraße 24, 80331 München, Germany

www.ingramcontent.com/pod-product-compliance
Lightning Source LLC
Chambersburg PA
CBHW070716220326
41598CB00024BA/3186